Heaven's Splendor

SR. MARY ANN FATULA, O.P.

HEAVEN'S
Splendor

And the Riches
That Await You There

SOPHIA INSTITUTE PRESS
Manchester, New Hampshire

Sophia Institute Press
Box 5284, Manchester, NH 03108
1-800-888-9344

www.SophiaInstitute.com

Sophia Institute Press® is a registered trademark of Sophia Institute.

Library of Congress Cataloging-in-Publication Data
To come

First printing

I dedicate this small work to the glory of the Trinity and in gratitude to my beloved mom and dad, who, I pray and trust, are now enjoying the wonders of heaven.

Contents

Introduction

Heaven. What an amazing word, intimating depths of joy we can only begin to imagine here on earth. If the mere word is so alluring, what must the reality be? Heaven is everything for which we are made, the answer to our inmost yearnings, the fulfillment of our deepest desires.

Though the human mind alone cannot fathom heaven's splendor, we can glimpse its magnificence through the insights of the saints. Their writings have the fragrant anointing of the Holy Spirit, who authored the Scriptures from which the saints draw their wisdom. Along with their reflections on heaven, gained from meditating on scriptural passages interpreted in union with the Church, the saints also offer us precious meditations on the mystical life of grace here on earth. These writings, too, give us profound insights on heaven's joy.

In this book, we ponder the depth and beauty of the saints' perceptions about heaven. If, as St. Paul assures us, the joys of heaven are beyond all that our minds can now imagine (1 Cor. 2:9), it is also impossible truly to contemplate these joys in a hurried manner. Rather than inviting us to a quick read of their insights, the saints draw us to a prayerful pondering of their words in the depths of our souls. They invite us to return again and again to their writings to understand more deeply and to savor more fully the beautiful truths about which they write. As we ponder their insights, we can feel the warmth of the saints' love for us, encouraging us to contemplate with them the joys of heaven and to deepen our desire to share in the delight that now fills them.

In the following chapters, with the saints' guidance, we will consider first the very heart of heaven, our sharing in the ecstatic love and life of the Blessed Trinity. We will reflect next on the marvelous Communion of Saints, whose love and tenderness we experience here on earth and hope to enjoy forever in heaven. In the third chapter, we will ponder the mysteries of our glorious resurrection, for we have been created to share, body as well as soul, in the joys of heaven. We will then turn to the mystery of death, which the Lord has transformed by His own death and Resurrection into our beautiful gateway into heaven. Finally, we will contemplate how we can begin to live in heaven even now, by adoring the Blessed Trinity dwelling in our souls, by receiving the precious Body and Blood of the Lord in the Eucharist, and by growing in the heavenly virtue of charity.

"Mary treasured all these words and pondered them in her heart" (Luke 2:19). May our Blessed Mother be our helper and guide as we consider these beautiful insights of the saints. Even now, we are surrounded by this great "cloud of witnesses" (Heb. 12:1) who long for us to share in their bliss. May we feel their closeness to us, and may the Holy Spirit, who anointed them, deepen our longing for heaven. May each of us be blessed one day to join our loved ones and all the angels and saints as they delight in the Divine Persons who are the very heart of heaven.

Heaven's Splendor

1

Delighting in the Trinity

We have been made for heaven; every fiber of our being longs for
it. Everything that brings us true and lasting delight on earth we
are created to possess beyond all our imagining in heaven: "No eye
has seen nor ear heard ... what God has prepared for those who
love Him" (1 Cor. 2:9). But what has God prepared for us? An
unending life of feasting on nothing less than God: "This is eternal
life, that they may know you, the only true God" (John 17:3).

We know by faith that God is not a solitary figure but the intimate communion of three Divine Persons: the Father, the Son,
and the Holy Spirit, who cherish us more dearly than our hearts
can conceive and who alone can satisfy our inmost longing for love.

Every one of us has been created to need and to have the most
perfect love. Regardless of how much we may be loved or may
long to be loved by other human beings, their love, as beautiful
as it is, can never be enough for us. The Persons of the Trinity
have created us to feast on *Their* love. They are every joy that
could possibly enchant us, every good our hearts could ever want.
Beholding the Trinity, we will see beauty itself; possessing the
Trinity, we will feast on infinite delight.[1]

---

[1] St. Thomas Aquinas, "Life Everlasting," in *Commentary on the
Apostles' Creed.*

"Enter into the joy" of your Lord! (Matt. 25:21). Heaven means being engulfed in the tremendous joy of the Trinity, surrounding and penetrating us, absorbing us as into a limitless ocean. We will enter into the ecstasy of the Father, the Son, and the Holy Spirit, who embrace us with the most exquisite love and draw us into Their intimate communion. We will be welcomed into the great throng of the angels and saints, who are jubilantly praising the Father, glorifying the Lord Jesus, and rejoicing in the Holy Spirit. The Trinity's happiness will be ours as we share in the very joy that the Divine Persons have in one another.[2]

Heaven Is the Blessed Trinity

It is impossible for us creatures to envision by our own powers the bliss that awaits us in heaven. Only the Divine Persons can reveal to us the mystery of Their love and the heavenly delight that will be ours in sharing Their love in heaven. For divine help in contemplating the mystery of the Trinity's ecstasy, the saints have begged, first of all, for the grace and anointing of the Holy Spirit. They have also turned to Scripture, inspired by the Holy Spirit, especially the Gospel of John, the beloved disciple who rested on the heart of the Lord at the Last Supper (see John 13:23). In this Gospel, Jesus calls us His beloved friends: "I have called you friends, because I have made known to you everything that I have heard from my Father" (John 15:15).[3] To John, the apostle and friend so intimately loved by Jesus (John 21:20),

---

[2] St. Thomas Aquinas, *Summa Theologiae* III.23.1.
[3] St. Thomas Aquinas, *Commentary on the Gospel of John*, prologue, no. 11, trans. Fabian Larcher, O.P., and James A. Weisheipl, O.P. (Albany, NY: Magi Books, 1980), Priory of the Immaculate Conception at the Dominican House of Studies, https://dhspriory.org/thomas/SSJohn.htm.

the Lord confided secrets of the Divine Persons' intimate love for one another, and thus of our heavenly joy in being received into Their embrace.

The saints have meditated on John's Gospel as it speaks of the infinite love among the three Divine Persons of the Trinity, the love in which we will share for all eternity. St. John Chrysostom comments that, rather than hearing simple tales from the "uneducated fisherman," John, we hear, instead, the most sublime, "heavenly things." The Evangelist writes as if he has been in heaven, and when we read his words, we feel as if we are in heaven.[4] John is the Gospel writer who tells us that, from all eternity, the beloved Son dwells in the tender depths of His Father's "bosom" (see John 1:18). There, with indescribable love, the Father eternally gives Himself to His Son: "The Father loves the Son and has placed all things in his hands" (John 3:35); "All that the Father has is Mine.... The Father and I are one" (John 16:15; 10:30). Wondrous mystery of love! From all eternity, the Father, fountain of all self-giving, gives all that He is, His divine nature, to His only-begotten, beloved Son, His equal. And the Son, eternally receiving all that He is from His Father, forever gives Himself completely to His Father in return.[5]

"No one knows the Son except the Father, and no one knows the Father except the Son and anyone to whom the Son chooses to reveal him" (Matt. 11:27). "I am in the Father" (John 14:11).

---

[4] St. John Chrysostom, *Commentary on Saint John the Apostle and Evangelist: Homilies 1–47*, Homily 2 (John 1:1), trans. Sister Thomas Aquinas Goggin, S.C.H. (New York: Fathers of the Church, 1957), pp. 13, 14.

[5] St. Thomas Aquinas, *Commentary on the Gospel of John*, chap. 1, lect. 11, no. 218; chap. 5, lect. 3, no. 753.

With exquisite insight, St. John of the Cross tells us that this
is the intimate mystery of love in which we will share forever
in heaven. Whether we realize it or not, our own deepest desire
is to live in the tender embrace of the Father, where the Son
eternally has His home. This, our hearts' longing, is fulfilled in
heaven beyond all that we could imagine. Dwelling in Jesus, we
will find our ecstasy in being infinitely cherished by the Father
in His "bosom," where the Son eternally dwells.[6]

In this way, we will dwell also in the Holy Spirit, who is the
"sweet Embrace" of the Father and the Son. Meditating on the
third Divine Person, who is the Spirit of the Father (see Matt.
10:20; John 15:26) and the Spirit of the Son (see Gal. 4:6), St.
Augustine contemplates the wondrous identity of the Holy Spirit
as the Father's and the Son's living Bond of Love.[7] Saints have
been struck with wonder before this sweet mystery of the Holy
Spirit, who, as the Father's and Son's inexpressible enjoyment and
bliss is also Their intoxicating perfume and exquisite delight. The
Father's and the Son's wondrous embrace is the Holy Spirit, whose
very name is joy. As the living love and delight of the Father and
the Son, the Holy Spirit, Their "sweetness,"[8] eternally receives
as Their equal all that He is from the Father and from the Son.[9]

St. Bernard tells us that the Holy Spirit, the eternal bond
of love between the Father and the Son, is also Their intimate

6 St. John of Cross, *The Spiritual Canticle* I.5, in *The Collected Works of St. John of the Cross*, trans. Kieran Kavanaugh, O.C.D., and Otilio Rodriguez, O.C.D. (Washington, D.C.: Institute of Carmelite Studies, 1973), p. 418.

7 St. Augustine, *On the Trinity* 15.17.27.

8 Ibid., 6.10.11.

9 St. Thomas Aquinas, *Commentary on the Gospel of John*, chap. 16, lect. 4, no. 2107.

"kiss," the highest kiss beyond all words. The love with which the Father eternally "embraces" His Son, and with which the Son eternally returns His Father's embrace, is Their tender Holy Spirit, Their "sweetest and most mysterious 'kiss.'" By eternally pouring into His Son all the mysteries of His divinity, the Father eternally "kisses" Him and "breathes the sweetness of love" in an eternal embrace of His beloved Son.[10]

This is the mystery that will enthrall us forever in heaven. Every dearest love story on earth, every experience of true and devoted love that we have been blessed to enjoy, is only a shadow and foretaste of this unfathomable love of the Divine Persons for one another. Every love that is good and beautiful has its source in this mystery of Trinitarian communion, in the infinite, self-giving love of the Divine Persons for one another. "O eternal Trinity," St. Catherine of Siena cries out, "you are a deep sea. The more I enter you, the more I discover, and the more I discover, the more I seek you.... My soul long[s] ... to see you."[11]

The psalmist sings, "Let your face shine, that we may be saved" (Ps. 80:3). St. Thomas Aquinas tells us that when we see someone "face-to-face," our vision reaches to the very depths of what we see and fills us with joy-filled love. "We will see Him as He is" (1 John 3:2). In heaven, we will gaze forever on the love and glory of the Trinity in a vision that will never exhaust the Trinity's magnificence but will forever satisfy our deepest longings.[12]

---

[10] St. Bernard of Clairvaux, *Sermons on the Song of Songs* 8.I.1 and 8.VI.6, in *Bernard of Clairvaux: Selected Works*, trans. G. E. Evans (New York: Paulist Press, 1987), pp. 236, 239.

[11] St. Catherine of Siena, *The Dialogue* 167, trans. Suzanne Noffke, O.P. (New York: Paulist Press, 1980), p. 364.

[12] St. Thomas Aquinas, *Summa Theologiae*, Supp. 92, 1.

"You shall *see*, and your heart shall rejoice!" (Isa. 66:14). The very heart of heaven is this Beatific Vision of the Trinity.[13] Love brings us to this vision, and love is its perfection. The fulfillment of our every desire is the supreme delight caused not by our physical sight, which can never behold what is infinite, but by an intellectual "seeing." By means of the Trinity's own divine essence, we will behold the Divine Persons' love and beauty with our intellects, in a vision that will fill us forever with ecstatic love.[14] This is the very purpose for which the Divine Persons have created us: that we may share intimately in this rapturous mystery of Their self-giving love for one another.

Our Closeness in Heaven to the Father

In heaven we will delight in distinct, marvelous ways in our unique closeness to each Person of the Most Blessed Trinity. Because the Father is the first Divine Person, the very font of all self-giving, we will find our joy first of all in His embrace. At the Last Supper, the Lord made this beautiful promise to us: "When I go and prepare a place for you, I will come again and will take you to myself, that where I am you may be also" (John 14:3). The Lord has His own dearest dwelling in the "bosom" of His Father (John 1:18), and nothing less than the Lord's own home will be ours forever in heaven.[15]

This is all the more a wondrous gift to us because the precious name "Father" contains the mystery of the Father's love, not first

---

[13] St. Thomas Aquinas, *Commentary on the Gospel of John*, chap. 17, lect. 1, no. 2186.

[14] St. Thomas Aquinas, *Summa Theologiae*, Supp. 92.1 ad. 3, 8.

[15] St. Augustine, *Tractates on the Gospel of John: 55–111*, 70.1; St. Thomas Aquinas, *Commentary on the Gospel of John*, chap. 14, lect. 1, no. 1856.

of all for us, but for His beloved Son.[16] It is the Son alone whose Father by nature is the first Divine Person. The divine name "Father" thus intimates the mystery of infinite self-giving to His only-begotten Son by eternally begetting Him as His equal. So, too, the divine name "Son" connotes the mystery of utterly selfless receiving from His beloved Father.[17] Through infinite love for us, the Father has chosen us to share in this wondrous mystery. We who by nature are only creatures have received through Baptism the precious gift of adoption as the Father's beloved sons and daughters in His own Son (Gal. 3:26; Rom. 8:15). As members of His Mystical Body, we dwell "in" the Son — "I am in my Father, and you in me" (John 14:20) — and are embraced by His Father as His very own sons and daughters in Jesus: "When you pray, say, 'Our Father'" (see Luke 11:2).

Thomas the Apostle had begged the Lord, "Show us the Father, and we will be satisfied" (John 14:8). What beautiful words! Our way to heaven is the Lord (John 14:6), but our ultimate destiny is dwelling in the Lord's own home, the tender depths of His beloved Father (John 1:18). The Lord Himself calls heaven "my Father's house" (John 14:2). St. Thomas Aquinas comments that heaven is not only the Father's "house" but, even more, the Father Himself.[18]

Our heavenly joy will thus be the ecstasy of dwelling with the Lord in the tender depths of His very own Father, the infinite fountain of self-giving and the source of all that is good (see James 1:17).[19] Overflowing with worship, adoration, and

---

[16] St. Thomas Aquinas, *Commentary on the Gospel of John*, chap. 2, lect. 2, no. 39.
[17] Ibid., chap. 15, lect. 4, no. 2112.
[18] Ibid., chap. 14, lect. 1, no. 1853.
[19] Ibid., chap. 14, lect. 2, no. 1875; lect. 3, no. 1883.

praise before the mystery of the Father's glory and love, our whole being will exult to behold the Father's beauty. We will delight forever in His wondrous embrace, as the Holy Spirit within us inspires us to cry out: "Abba, Father!" (Rom. 8:15; Gal. 4:6). There, in the Father's arms, our every ache to know fully and completely who we are, and whose we are, will be completely satisfied.

As members of His Son's Mystical Body, we will delight to hear His Father say tenderly to *us*: "My beloved daughter" or "My beloved son" (see Mark 1:11; Matt. 3:17). We will thrill with joy as we grasp the mystery of our identity and purpose in the Father's heart. In His tender embrace, every one of us will savor also the irreplaceable blessing we were created to be. We will see with utter clarity that no one is a mistake and that every one of us was created to be unique in all of history. With ecstatic joy, we will ceaselessly thank the Father for treasuring us as His own precious children, for freely choosing and unconditionally loving us from all eternity.

How deeply our whole being will bow in adoration before the Father's infinite love and glory! With unbounded joy, we will praise Him for so tenderly providing for our every need, for protecting us with infinitely sweet and fierce love. What gratitude will fill us as we realize how the Father has never ceased to hold us close, caring for us more gently than the most loving mother nurses her child at her breast: "You shall nurse and be carried on her arm. As a mother comforts her child, so I will comfort you" (Isa. 66:12–13).

St. John of the Cross tells us of an even greater mystery: with profound humility and sweetness, the Father will give Himself, completely surrender Himself, to us, as if He were our slave and we were His God. The Lord Jesus promised that in heaven He

Himself will serve us (Luke 12:37). He also assures us: "Whoever has seen me, has seen the Father" (John 14:9). The mystery of the Father giving Himself to us and forever serving us will impart to us an intimate sharing in the exquisite mystery of the Father's eternal giving of Himself to His beloved Son.[20]

"No one knows the Son except the Father, and no one knows the Father except the Son and anyone to whom the Son chooses to reveal him" (Matt. 11:27). Because the Father wants us to know Him and His unfathomable love for us intimately, He has given us His own Son to "captivate" us.[21] Enclosed in His Son, we will dwell forever in the tender arms of our very own Father, where every longing of our hearts to be infinitely loved and treasured will be satisfied beyond all that we could ask or imagine.

Our Closeness in Heaven to the Lord Jesus

In heaven, we will realize the depths of the Father's love for us in giving us every good, and, most of all, in not withholding from us even His only beloved Son (see John 3:16). Forever we will delight, therefore, not only in the Father but also in His Son, who, through infinite love for His Father and for us, gave Himself unreservedly to us, completely sacrificing Himself for our sake. After His death and Resurrection, the Lord spoke these beautiful words to Mary Magdalene and, through her, to His apostles and to each one of us: "I am ascending to my Father and *your* Father" (John 20:17). In His glorious, risen body, the Lord returned to His most wondrous home, the Father's bosom,[22] where He now

---

[20] St. John of the Cross, *The Spiritual Canticle* 27.1, p. 517.
[21] St. Thomas Aquinas, *Commentary on the Gospel of John*, chap. 6, lect. 5, no. 935.
[22] St. John of the Cross, The *Spiritual Canticle* I.5, pp. 417–418.

reigns in glory.[23] And where the Lord dwells, He wants to bring us: "I desire that those also, whom you have given me, may be with me where I am, to see my glory" (John 17:24).

Dwelling forever in the Father, we thus will savor also the divine glory of His beloved Son: "Your eyes will see the king in his beauty!" (Isa. 33:17). In a special way, we will gaze with wonder on the glory of the Lord's risen body, radiating a beauty so wondrous that, as St. John Chrysostom assures us, no words could ever describe it. "O blessed many times over [are] they who are deemed worthy to become beholders of that glory! Why do we exist, if we fail to obtain that sight?"[24] How ceaseless will be our praise of the Lord for freely enduring the most horrendous suffering for our sake, suffering by which He gained the glorious splendor of His risen body. We will never tire of thanking the Lord for choosing to be born in a stable among the animals, enduring freezing cold for us. At the end of His life, He allowed Himself to be scourged, beaten, blasphemed, crucified, and pierced with a lance. To free and heal us of all our sins, He let His precious blood pour out from His hands and feet and side like a sacred bath.[25]

We will cherish in heaven these depths of the Lord's love in becoming man for our sake, choosing to suffer unimaginable pain on the Cross for our salvation.[26] We will never stop praising Him for making present His sacred Passion, death, and Resurrection in every Mass, and for giving us His own precious Body and Blood

---

[23] St. Thomas Aquinas, *Commentary on the Gospel of John*, chap. 16, lect. 7, no. 2163.

[24] St. John Chrysostom, *Commentary on Saint John the Apostle and Evangelist*, Homily 12 (John 1:14), p. 118.

[25] St. Catherine of Siena, *The Dialogue* 151, p. 320.

[26] Ibid.

in the Eucharist to nourish us unto eternal life. What gratitude will fill us as we fully realize all that the Lord Jesus endured for us, so that, in Him, our own wounds and sufferings could be transformed into bliss.

With wonder and awe we will glorify the Lord as we gaze on His sacred wounds, suffered for our sake, wounds now shining gloriously from His risen body. He was crucified, and His side was "pierced with a spear" (John 19:34). Through the openings of these wounds, we will drink "honey from the rock" and will forever "taste and see that the LORD is good" (Ps 81:16; 34:8). With great tenderness, St. Bernard contemplates the sweetness of these wounds, where we will find the most exquisite peace. In them we will find unveiled the secret of the Lord's heart, the great mystery of His infinite love for each of us.[27] What gratitude will fill us as we truly understand the meaning of St. Paul's words: the Lord "loved *me* and gave Himself for *me*" (Gal. 2:20).

Most of all, every part of our being will bow in adoration before the Lord as we finally grasp the wondrous truth that He is not only our Savior but also our tender Spouse. The Lord calls Himself our "Bridegroom" (see Matt. 9:15; 25:1–13; Mark 2:20; Luke 5:35) who loves each one of us with a unique, exclusive love. Through His precious suffering and death for us, He has tenderly brought us into His heavenly "bridal chamber." An early Christian homily on Holy Saturday depicts the Lord, our Spouse (see Rev. 21:9), after His death coming to Adam and Eve, who languish in the place of the dead. The Lord greets them with infinite love: "You are in me, and I am in you; together we form only one person. See the marks of the scourging I endured to

---

[27] St. Bernard of Clairvaux, "Sermon 61 on the Song of Songs," no. 4.

remove your sin. The bridal chamber is adorned, the banquet is ready."[28]

"Blessed are they who are invited to the marriage supper of the Lamb" (Rev. 19:9). Yes, heaven is our bridal chamber, as well as our true and lasting wedding banquet, forever celebrating our heavenly marriage to the Lord Jesus, our Divine Spouse. The Gospel account of the wedding feast at Cana (John 2:1–11) in a profound way refers to this mystical marriage of the Lord with each one of us, a marriage begun at the Incarnation and destined to be consummated in heaven. There we will be embraced by Jesus our Spouse forever.[29]

In heaven, all of our desires to be loved with an intimate love will thus be fulfilled beyond all that we could imagine. Having longed for such a love on earth, each of us will receive in the tender embrace of the Lord Jesus, who is the divine Spouse of each of us, man or woman, the fulfillment of our every longing to be exclusively loved. This is the deepest reason why there is no marriage between human beings in heaven (Mark 12:25; Matt. 22:30), though surely the unique closeness between spouses remains forever, immeasurably deepened and far more sweet and precious.[30] The dearest married love on earth offers us only a foretaste of and sharing in this spousal love for which we are truly made and which alone can satisfy every craving of our

---

[28] See "An Ancient Homily on Holy Saturday," The Liturgy Archive, http://www.liturgies.net/Liturgies/Catholic/loh/lent/holysaturdayor.htm..

[29] St. Thomas Aquinas. *Commentary on the Gospel of John*, chap. 2, lect. 1, no. 337.

[30] St. John Paul II, General Audience (December 16, 1981); St. Catherine of Siena, *The Dialogue* 41, p. 33.

hearts for closeness: the infinite love of the Lord Jesus, our divine Bridegroom.

St. John Paul II stresses that our most profound meaning as human beings, composed of soul and body, truly is spousal: we were created as man or woman to be unreserved "gift." This vocation at the very depths of who we are is perfectly realized only in heaven, where we will experience in an unhindered way the rapturous joy of the Lord's unreserved self-giving to us: "All [that is] mine is yours" (John 17:10). The Lord will surrender Himself completely and uniquely to each of us as our Spouse, and, in His love, we will completely surrender ourselves to Him.[31] This mutual self-giving and communion between the Lord and us will satiate us with indescribable delight and fill us with profound gratitude that the Lord is so "captivated" by us.[32] Placing us in honor at His side, the Lord will show each one of us to all of heaven as the "crown and joy of His heart," His precious spouse and "equal" through love forever.[33]

Our Closeness in Heaven to the Holy Spirit

The mystery of love: this is the heart of heaven. As we have seen, however, love is not only the divine nature of the three Persons of the Trinity; love also is a Person, the Holy Spirit, the living bond of love between the Father and Son. St. Luke describes the tremendous day of Pentecost, when the Holy Spirit descended with power and tenderness upon crowds of strangers whom He made "one heart and soul" (Acts 4:32). This miracle occurred through the wondrous activity of the Holy Spirit, who set them

---

[31] St. John Paul II, General Audience (December 16, 1981).
[32] St. John of the Cross, *The Spiritual Canticle* 31.9–10, p. 534.
[33] Ibid., 22.1; 30.6, pp. 496, 528.

aflame with love (Acts 2:3) because He is the very fountain of love.[34]

St. Augustine was deeply moved by the inspired words of St. Paul: "God's love has been poured into our hearts through the Holy Spirit that has been given to us" (Rom. 5:5). As he meditated on the mystery of the Father eternally loving the Son, and the Son eternally returning His Father's love, St. Augustine was inspired to speak of the Holy Spirit as the exquisite divine Person who is Their mutual love.[35] Love that cherishes us for who we are, love that desires and works only for our good, love that completely transforms us: Is this not the gift for which every one of us longs? It is love that strengthens, consoles, and delights us, and these very blessings are ours through the Holy Spirit of love poured out upon us at our Baptisms and dwelling intimately within us (1 Cor. 3:16).

How great will be our joy in heaven as the Holy Spirit unveils to us all the wondrous ways He filled us with His sweet strength and consolation on earth (Acts 9:31), often without our realizing it. We will finally grasp the countless miracles of love He accomplished for us and within us. Our wonder will have no bounds as we see how tenderly the Holy Spirit was always with us, guiding us (John 14:16, 26) and filling us with His peace, love, and joy (Gal. 5:22), especially in difficult and painful times (Acts 13:52; 1 Thess. 1:6).

In heaven, we will gaze with awe on the beauty of this Divine Person, who, as supreme love, is also glorious gift (Acts 2:38; 13:52). Lavishly poured out on us (Rom. 5:5) by the Father and Son as Their precious gift, the Holy Spirit also will give Himself

---

[34] St. Augustine, *Tractates on the Gospel of John: 28–54*, 39.4.1, trans. John W. Rettig (Washington, D.C.: Catholic University of America Press, 1993), p. 120.

[35] St. Augustine, *On the Trinity* 15.17.27; 15.19.37.

to us without reserve.[36] Love itself is the first gift, for all that we freely bestow on a loved one is given out of love, and what is given ultimately is our love. This is why we want our loved one truly to possess and to enjoy our gift. St. Thomas Aquinas uses these beautiful insights to illumine how wondrously the Holy Spirit is the gift we are created to possess and enjoy here on earth and ever more gloriously in heaven.[37] There, the Holy Spirit will give Himself completely to us, to "belong" to us, to be "possessed" by us forever.[38] This precious blessing is already ours through sanctifying grace, but what ecstatic delight will fill us when we savor in an unhindered way the Holy Spirit's sweetness in heaven!

"Let him kiss me with the kisses of his mouth" (Song of Sol. 1:2). In these beautiful words of Scripture, St. Bernard of Clairvaux recognized the exquisite mystery of the Holy Spirit not only as the Father's and Son's love and gift, but also as Their sweetest and most sublime "kiss." From all eternity, the Father "kisses" His beloved Son, and His Son receives and returns His Father's kiss. The Holy Spirit is Their kiss, the most intimate "secret" of Their love.[39] In a wondrous way, the Risen Lord shared this most sweet kiss with His beloved apostles: "Receive the Holy Spirit" (John 20:22). We ourselves receive this precious kiss through the outpouring or deepening of sanctifying grace in our souls.[40] Furthermore, deep within us, the Holy Spirit Himself is constantly "kissing" us with His tenderness even when we are

---

[36] Ibid., 15.17.29; 15.18.32; 15.19.33–35.

[37] St. Thomas Aquinas, *Summa Theologiae* I.38.1, 2.

[38] Ibid., I.38.1, 2; 43.3.

[39] St. Bernard of Clairvaux, *Sermons on the Song of Songs* 8.I.1, in *Bernard of Clairvaux: Selected Works*, trans. G. E. Evans (New York: Paulist Press, 1987), p. 236.

[40] Ibid., 8.I.2, p. 237.

unaware of His dear presence within us. In heaven, however, the Holy Spirit will kiss us with a sweetness that we will fully savor with every fiber of our being.[41]

St. John of the Cross tells us that the Father and the Son will also share with us in heaven Their most intimate activity, Their eternal breathing forth of their Holy Spirit. "Father, I desire that those also, whom you have given me, may be with me where I am" (John 17:24). St. John interprets this beautiful passage to mean, "Father, may the ones You have given me share in the sacred mystery of our love, our eternal breathing forth of the Holy Spirit, who is Our love." This heavenly blessing will give us an intimacy with the Holy Spirit "so sublime, delicate, and deep" that its delight is impossible even to imagine.[42]

In the beautiful Sequence for the Mass of Pentecost, we pray to the Holy Spirit who is our intimate Comforter, our souls' "Most Welcome Guest," our "Sweet Refreshment" here on earth. We beg the Holy Spirit, giver of all joy, to give us His strength, to pour His sweet dew on our parched souls (see Acts 13:52). In heaven, we will see clearly what we so often fail to recognize here on earth: it is the Holy Spirit who gently heals our every wound, who strengthens us in every trial, and who tenderly comforts us in every sorrow. Inwardly teaching us, illumining the mysteries of our Faith for us, leading and guiding us when every road seems closed to us, the Holy Spirit draws us even now to heaven's joy through every experience of our lives.[43] In heaven, we will feast without hindrance on this tenderness of the

---

[41] Ibid., 8.IV.6, p. 239.
[42] St. John of the Cross, *The Living Flame of Love* 4.17, in *Collected Works*, p. 649; *The Spiritual Canticle* 39.3, p. 558.
[43] St. Thomas Aquinas, *Summa Theologiae* I-II.68.2.

Delighting in the Trinity

Holy Spirit, filling us with the most exquisite consolation (see Gal. 5:22)[44] and flooding our souls with a "torrent of delight."[45]

The Trinity, Our Heavenly Family and Home

In Andrei Rublev's beautiful icon of the Trinity, the Divine Persons, imaged in the three angelic figures who visited Abraham and Sarah (Gen. 18:1–15), are seated around a banquet table of Their love, which They invite us to share now through the Eucharist, and forever in heaven. How great will be our heavenly joy to share fully in the intimate love of the Blessed Trinity, our true Family, by whom and for whom we were created, and to whom we most deeply, irrevocably belong. We will be filled with gratitude for the grace of sharing in the Divine Persons' love for one another.[46] Inflamed by the Trinity's love, we will return unreservedly to the Divine Persons the only gift worthy of Them: Themselves. Sharing in the Trinity's own love, we will love the Trinity with all that we are, cherishing the Father, the Son, and the Holy Spirit fully in return.[47]

The best and most wonderful delights we experience here on earth are only a taste of this exquisite joy that will be ours as we share fully in the self-giving love of the Trinity. With Our Blessed Mother, the angels, and the saints, we will sing forever in praise of the Divine Persons who are worthy of all our worship, love, and praise. Placed in the very center of our beloved Divine Family in heaven, we will find ourselves finally in our own true home. The Father will embrace us in His love, Jesus will hold

---

[44] St. Thomas Aquinas, *Commentary on the Gospel of John*, chap. 14, lect. 4, no. 1910.
[45] St. John of the Cross, *The Spiritual Canticle* 26.1, p. 511.
[46] Ibid., 32.6, p. 536.
[47] St. John of the Cross, *The Living Flame of Love* 3.78, p. 641.

us close to His heart, and the Holy Spirit will bathe our soul in His tenderness. Dwelling in the "splendid sweetness" of the Trinity, we will rejoice to be received into the Divine Persons' unending "exchange of sweet love."[48] This truly is the heavenly rapture for which we have been made: being engulfed forever in the tender and intimate love of our own true Family, the most sweet Blessed Trinity.[49]

---

[48] St. John of the Cross, *The Spiritual Canticle* 14–15, 4; 14–15, 2, pp. 464, 463.
[49] St. Gregory of Nazianzus, *Oration 8: On His Sister, St. Gorgonia* 23.

2

Enjoying the Communion of Saints

"I believe in the Communion of Saints." What heavenly joy these words of the Apostles' Creed convey! Our ecstasy in heaven is delighting in the Trinity, but the Divine Persons' infinite love for us also gives us the precious gift of one another.

The virtue of charity is the heart of the wondrous Communion of Saints by which the Trinity, in Their selfless love, bind us to each other here on earth. It also joins us to the saints and the angels in heaven and to all those who have died in the grace of the Lord, especially our families and loved ones, so tenderly created in the image of the self-giving Trinity. One tremendous dimension of this Communion of Saints is that death, which seems to be a final goodbye, is, in fact, the beginning of an entirely new and wonderful way of our being close to our dear ones who have died. It is true that the angels and all the blessed await "with great joy and gladness" our joining them in heaven, but they also are very near to us even now, never ceasing to love us and to come to our aid.[50]

---

[50] St. Catherine of Siena, *The Dialogue* 147, p. 310.

The Communion of Saints
in the Bond of Charity

Charity is patient and kind; it does not come to an end (see 1 Cor. 13:4, 8). The very root of the Communion of Saints is the beautiful virtue of charity. "Poured into our hearts through the Holy Spirit" (Rom. 5:5) at our Baptisms, charity is the greatest of all the virtues (1 Cor. 13:13) because it unites us intimately to the Trinity.[51] As a created share in the Trinity's divine love, however, charity also unites us irrevocably to one another. The Trinity bind us together by the gentle "chain" of charity, which gives us the power and the desire to love and help one another. Because "charity does not come to an end," this most beautiful of all the virtues continues beyond death and unites us to each other forever.[52] Even now, we are invisibly surrounded by a "great cloud of witnesses" (Heb. 12:1), those who have died in the Lord's grace and who continue to love us, to be near us, and to come to our aid. In a continual "exchange of spiritual goods," they help and pray for us, just as we on earth pray to and for those who have died.[53] The Divine Persons delight in this charity, which extends across death and which we show in our prayers for and to one another.

We put this Trinitarian love into practice here on earth when, in the Communion of Saints, we help others in their need, and, most of all, when we pray for one another. Since the earliest centuries of Christianity, the Church has had the beautiful practice of offering prayers for those who have died, having Masses celebrated for them, and praying for them at every Mass. It is a

---

[51] St. Thomas Aquinas, *Summa Theologiae* II-II.23.6.
[52] St. Catherine of Siena, *The Dialogue* 148, p. 312.
[53] *Catechism of the Catholic Church* (hereafter CCC), no. 955.

"holy and pious thought" to pray for the dead, "that they might be delivered from their sin" (2 Macc. 12:45). We believe that our prayers truly benefit those who have died and who may be undergoing purgatory's purifying love.[54]

This same charity uniting us to one another in the Communion of Saints also inspires us to bury our loved ones in cemeteries whose ground has been consecrated, and the very holiness of the grounds encourages us to pray for them. The Divine Persons of the Trinity are glorified in this way by our being, in Their self-giving love and grace, the cause of unceasing goodness and kindness toward one another, even across the boundaries of death. As our pledge and foretaste even now of heaven's sweet "life together," the charity at the heart of the Communion of Saints truly never comes to an end (1 Cor. 13:8).[55]

The Blessed in Heaven Are with Us

The bonds of love that the Trinity have formed among us on earth thus do not end at death, nor do those we have loved on earth abandon us when they die. They are still with us, and more dearly than ever. We can speak to them and enjoy their sweet embrace deep in our souls. We can be comforted by their presence, be guided by their wisdom, and experience their help in our every need. They are close to us and most of all to the Trinity, who bless their charity by answering in wonderful ways their constant prayer for us.[56] Although we do not see them with our eyes, we can experience the power of our deceased loved ones'

---

[54] St. Thomas Aquinas, *Summa Theologiae*, Supp. 71.1.
[55] Ibid., 71.9, 11.
[56] St. Gregory of Nazianzus, *Oration 18: On His Father* 4.

prayers and help, for "in whatever bond of love they finish their lives, that bond is theirs forever."[57]

Many of the saints tell us of their experience of the invisible, loving presence of their dear family members and other loved ones who died. St. Gregory of Nazianzus writes that after the death of his dear friend St. Basil, he felt Basil's constant help and counsel.[58] St. Ambrose of Milan gives us a precious account that encourages us to grow in our closeness to loved ones who have died. In a touching sermon praising his deceased brother Satyrus, to whom he was very close, Ambrose confesses that he very much grieved his brother's death, but he could not complain or be ungrateful, for his brother was a gift: "I enjoyed the loan entrusted to me. Now, He who deposited the pledge has taken it back." Every time his brother's name was mentioned, Ambrose would break into tears, and yet he was not ashamed to weep, for even the Lord wept (John 11:35). Deeper than his sorrow, however, was the comfort Ambrose felt in experiencing the far deeper closeness of his brother.[59]

This sense of his brother's nearness inspired Ambrose to speak these tender words directly to Satyrus: "I have not lost you; you remain with me, and ever will remain."[60] As Ambrose grew in his realization that his brother continued to be with him on earth, he himself began to live in some way in heaven, where, he trusted, his brother dwelt: "I begin to be no stranger there, where the better portion of myself already is."[61] Surely this is true also of us. The death of our loved ones, and our prayers that they are

[57] St. Catherine of Siena, *The Dialogue* 41, p. 84.

[58] St. Gregory of Nazianzus, *Oration 43: On St. Basil* 80.

[59] St. Ambrose, *On the Death of Satyrus* I.3, 10, 72.

[60] Ibid., I.6.

[61] Ibid.

in heaven, help to free us from the fear of death, filling us with trust that they will be with us to bring us gently home.

Sometimes our deceased loved ones may make known their deeper presence with us through dreams. St. Ambrose tells us that his dreams were so consoling to him that he looked forward to sleeping at night, when his brother would visit and comfort him. Thus, the mutual help they enjoyed on earth was not interrupted but rather deepened by his brother's death.[62] When he was complaining to his brother that his dreams of him were too infrequent, Ambrose realized that he did not need dreams to experience his closeness. "The enjoyment of each other which we were unable to have in this life is now always and everywhere with us." Ambrose asked Satyrus to console their sister, in order that she, too, would feel how much her brother was with her. Since they had shared deeply on earth, Ambrose also begged his brother to prepare a place for him in heaven so that they soon would have the joy of dwelling together forever: "Go before us to that home waiting for all, and now longed for by me beyond others. Prepare a common dwelling for me with whom you have dwelt" here.[63]

St. Catherine of Siena also encourages us to pray for deepened faith in the closeness of our deceased loved ones. When her father was dying, she begged the Lord that through her prayer and sacrifices he would be spared the purification of purgatory and would enter immediately into heaven's joy. At his death, she could only smile while others wept, because she believed that her prayer had been answered.[64] After her father's death,

---

[62] Ibid., I.6, 72.

[63] Ibid., I.77, 78.

[64] Bl. Raymond of Capua, *The Life of Catherine of Siena*, trans. Conleth Kearns, O.P. (Wilmington, DE: Michael Glazier, 1980) no. 368, p. 342.

Catherine often felt him close to her, thanking her for her love, prayers, and sacrifices, especially to help him enter into heaven. She also experienced him telling her many precious secrets and constantly protecting her.[65] Catherine's dear friend Raymond of Capua was not with her when she died, but after her death he heard her telling him to fear nothing, since she was constantly caring for him and keeping him safe from harm.[66]

St. Thérèse of Lisieux is another saint who gives us precious insights about the nearness of our deceased loved ones. She was very close to her family and said that she did not understand saints who do not speak about how dearly they love their relatives.[67] She had suffered greatly as a young child because of her mother's death, but when her older sister took on the role of caring for her, Thérèse realized that it was her dear mother in heaven who provided her sister's comfort and tenderness in her place.[68] Thérèse also grieved intensely because of the painful death of her beloved father, who had suffered from dementia. After his death, however, she experienced the grace of his constant nearness. "I feel him around me ... protecting me." Her mother's and father's closeness to her after their deaths deepened Thérèse's sense that, just as they continued to be with her on earth, in some way she also began to live with them in heaven.[69]

---

[65] Ibid., 222, p. 211.

[66] Ibid., 223, p. 212.

[67] St. Thérèse of Lisieux: Her Last Conversations, trans. John Clarke, O.C.D. (Washington, D.C.: ICS Publications, 1977), pp. 46–47.

[68] St. Thérèse of Lisieux, Letter 133, in Letters of St. Thérèse of Lisieux, vol. 2, trans. John Clarke, O.C.D. (Washington, D.C.: ICS Publications, 1988), p. 743.

[69] St. Thérèse of Lisieux, Letter 170, in Letters, vol. 2, p. 884.

Enjoying the Communion of Saints

Thérèse's experience is consoling in a special way to all of us who may have suffered the death of a parent, especially when we were young. Freed from all human frailty, our parents in heaven deeply love us and are constantly protecting and caring for us. They are intimately present at every precious occasion, at every celebration, even though we might have thought they were missing. They delight to share in our every joy and to comfort us in our every sorrow. Surely the experiences of such saints as Ambrose, Catherine, and Thérèse encourage us to rely ever more deeply on the constant help and protection of our own deceased loves ones.

Our Closeness to Saints We Have Never Met

Although everyone in heaven knows us and unfailingly smiles upon us, we are meant to enjoy also a special relationship with cherished saints in heaven whom we love as intimate friends but whom we have never met. The saints themselves have been granted this great blessing. St. Catherine of Siena was given a deep bond with St. Dominic, who had died two centuries before her, and who often visited her and shared with her the secrets of his heart. She said that she could see Dominic more clearly than she could see the person sitting next to her. Catherine also enjoyed a special friendship with another saint she had never met, St. Agnes of Montepulciano, who promised her that they would be close forever in heaven. The Lord gave Catherine a deep friendship also with St. Mary Magdalene. Knowing what it is to be weak, this saint taught Catherine to trust in the Lord's mercy in her frailty and trials.[70] Catherine's experience surely inspires us also to nurture the

---

[70] Bl. Raymond of Capua, *Life of Catherine* 202, 328, 183, 185, pp. 193, 303, 177, 179.

gift of a special relationship with cherished saints and to rely on their constant prayer and help.

Just as St. Thérèse treasured her family, she, too, enjoyed a closeness to saints in heaven whom she had never met. Blessed with a special love for St. Cecilia, the third-century saint whose tomb she had visited in Rome when she was an adolescent, Thérèse found in Cecilia a true sister, friend, and confidante. Realizing that we are constantly receiving the "caresses" of those in heaven, Thérèse tells us that the French Carmel's deceased foundress, whom she had never met, also became a beloved friend. After a special encounter with her, Thérèse was filled with joy, and, for a long time afterward, she felt the Sister's closeness to her. This tender experience convinced her of how much everyone in heaven loves us: "I felt that ... heaven is peopled with souls who actually love me, who consider me their child."[71] Certainly, Thérèse assures us that each one of us can make these precious words of hers our own.

Learning to thank and praise the Lord for everyone in heaven, Thérèse began to view the saints as our beloved "relatives." Knowing her weakness and the tremendous love of the saints and angels for us, Thérèse would pray in her needs to her own deceased little siblings, whom she had never met. When she was feeling anxious, Thérèse begged them to obtain for her the gift of serenity. When peace flooded her soul, she realized that it was they who had obtained this precious grace for her. "I knew then that if I was loved on earth, I was also loved in heaven. Since that moment,

---

[71] St. Thérèse of Lisieux, *Story of a Soul: The Autobiography of St. Thérèse of Lisieux*, trans. John Clarke, O.C.D. (Washington, D.C.: ICS Publications, 1972), pp. 131, 191; *Her Last Conversations*, p. 50.

my devotion for my little brothers and sisters has grown and I love to ... speak with them."[72]

What beautiful encouragement for those of us who have beloved children or grandchildren, brothers or sisters who died while in the womb or as little ones, or when we were too young to remember them.[73] Although we have not yet met them, they intimately know and love us. They are with us, tenderly sharing our burdens and helping us in our every trial. What joy it will be to meet them in heaven! This is why parents of unborn children who have died are encouraged to name their children, to speak to and pray to them, and to grow in their relationship with them. It is a wonderful grace to realize that there are saints in heaven, children and parents, grandparents, brothers and sisters, relatives and loving ancestors whom we have not yet met, but who constantly help us and await our homecoming with joy. They cherish us, pray for us, and help us in ways we could never have imagined. What gladness it will bring us to meet them in person and to feel their wonderful embrace and closeness in heaven!

There also awaits us a wonderful company of those in the Communion of Saints whom we do not yet know, but whom the Divine Persons have chosen to be especially close to us in heaven. Here on earth, life can bring us not only joys but also disappointments, wounds, and unfulfilled dreams. In heaven, however, no one feels deprived because of having lost or never having attained particular blessings on earth. Our dreams of having a loving family, close friends, a spouse to dearly love us, and children to bless

---

[72] St. Thérèse of Lisieux, *Story of a Soul*, p. 93.

[73] On our hope and trust that unbaptized babies are brought to heaven's joy through the merciful love of the Trinity, see page 37 of this chapter and CCC 1257 and 1261.

us will all be fulfilled through the Communion of Saints in a way more marvelous than we could have dreamed.

This very truth is beautifully illumined by St. John Paul II. We already have considered his profound insight that the Divine Persons of the Trinity have created us as man or woman so that we may be, even in our bodies, unreserved "gift," reflecting the self-giving love that the Divine Persons are. Every earthly love is but a foreshadowing of this measureless love of the Trinity, which alone can satisfy our hearts. In heaven, we will receive the tremendous grace of returning the Divine Persons' infinite self-giving to us in a reciprocal surrender that will fill every part of our being with unimaginable ecstasy. The further wonder, St. John Paul II tells us, is that this mutual self-giving between the Trinity and us will result in a magnificent, new, glorious closeness between us and those in heaven, in the perfect realization of the Communion of Saints.[74]

The implications of this profound communion with everyone in heaven are marvelous. Have we longed for a beloved spouse, a treasured child, an intimate friend, without ever having received these blessings on earth? Do we grieve losses and deprivations, loneliness and unfulfilled dreams? Do we mourn because someone we love seemed to die alone and unfulfilled? Through the Trinity's magnificent love for us, in the Communion of Saints we will be given a million times over every blessing of human love for which our hearts yearned on earth but never attained. At this very moment, saints in heaven, saints we know and saints we do not yet know, are waiting for us, loving us, looking forward to our coming home. There we will find in their special closeness to us a fulfillment that will heal every deprivation of human love that we may have experienced on earth.

---

[74] St. John Paul II, General Audience (December 16, 1981).

Enjoying the Communion of Saints

The Blessed in Heaven Constantly Help Us

As we have seen, our loved ones in the Communion of Saints are not taken away from us in death; they are intimately in our midst. But they are not idle. They love to pray and work on our behalf, just as they did when they lived on earth. Through all the ages, holy people have lived with great charity on earth, praying and laboring for others' good. Saints such as Catherine of Siena were filled with such "boundless love" for others that they would gladly have suffered anything, including death, if even one person could be brought to heaven by their self-giving love.[75] This great charity for us does not end with death. Our Blessed Mother, the angels, and all the blessed, including our loved ones, never stop praying for us and coming to our aid in every way possible. Having spent their lives loving and helping others, the saints in heaven do not "leave that love behind."[76]

Most of all, our Blessed Mother never ceases to pray for us and to come to our aid in our every need. "Here is your Mother" (John 19:27). The Lord has given His precious mother to every one of us. What tremendous joy it will be for us to see "face to face" in heaven the Mother of God, given to us to be our Mother, the one who is "more honorable than the Cherubim, beyond compare more glorious than the Seraphim."[77] Our Mother is so filled with kindness, tenderness, and love that no one who has asked for her intercession has ever been turned away. Her union

---

[75] Bl. Raymond of Capua, *Life of Catherine* 182, p. 176.
[76] St. Catherine of Siena, *The Dialogue* 41, p. 83.
[77] "Hymn to the Mother of God," Divine Liturgy of St. John Chrysostom, Byzantine Catholic Archeparchy of Pittsburgh, http://www.archpitt.org/prayers-to-the-blessed-mother-of-god-according-to-the-byzantine-rite-tradition/.

with her beloved Son is so perfect that He grants whatever she begs of Him.[78]

St. Catherine of Siena calls our Blessed Mother a "tree of mercy" so wounded by love for our salvation[79] that, if needed, she would have made of her own body a ladder by which her beloved Son could be put on the Cross.[80] Mary's immense love for us, her children, inspired St. John Damascene to cry out in gratitude to the Mother of God, "You are rest for the weary, consolation for the grieving, healing for the sick, a harbor for the storm-tossed ... ready help for all who call on you."[81]

Our Blessed Mother's constant help for us serves as a model and an inspiration for all of the blessed in heaven. So many of us have experienced in our need the aid of the saints, including our loved ones. St. Thérèse of Lisieux, who embodies every saint's concern for our welfare, meditated on how one small light can be shared and thus illumine an immense space. Contemplating how the Communion of Saints enables the smallest among us to be enriched by the greatest, Thérèse writes that the saints, filled with the Trinity's love, help and pray for us "with a love much greater than even the most perfect family on earth."[82]

Writing to her dear friend and spiritual brother Fr. Maurice Bellière, Thérèse promised that, after her death, she would be

[78] St. Louis de Montfort, *True Devotion to Mary* 85.

[79] St. Catherine of Siena, Letter 1, in *The Letters of St. Catherine of Siena*, vol. 1, trans. Suzanne Noffke, O.P. (Binghamton, NY: Medieval and Renaissance Texts and Studies, 1988), pp. 38–39.

[80] St. Catherine of Siena, Letter 34, in *Letters*, vol. 1, p. 118.

[81] St. John Damascene, "On the Dormition of the Mother of God," Homily 1, in *On the Dormition of Mary: Early Patristic Homilies*, trans. Brian E. Daley, S.J. (Crestwood, NY: St. Vladimir's Seminary Press, 1998), p. 196.

[82] St. Thérèse of Lisieux, *Her Last Conversations*, p. 99.

far more able to help those in need and that she would always be "very close" to him. Their union would not be broken by death but rather made stronger and more intimate: "You will know only in heaven how dear you are to me." "I shall be for all eternity your true little sister."[83] St. Thérèse surely speaks these precious words to each of us in the name of all the saints.

Thérèse assured another spiritual brother, Fr. Adolphe Roulland, that he would only have to whisper to her and she would hear him. At the moment of his death, she would be close to him and make his death easy and peaceful: "I shall be near you, holding your hand ... and then with joy we shall fly together into the heavenly homeland!"[84] This pledge of Thérèse encourages us to trust that our own loved ones also will be very close to us at the time of our death. They will not let us die alone. With the Trinity and our Blessed Mother, the angels and saints will be there to assist us as we die. In a very special way, our deceased loved ones will be present to pray for us, to comfort and strengthen us, and to hold us close. Many of us have known people who were dying and who experienced this consoling presence of deceased loved ones. Many of us, too, have been with dying loved ones who were aware of the loving presence of others invisible to us.

As she neared her death, Thérèse eagerly looked forward to beginning a wonderful mission from heaven: "I want to spend my heaven in doing good on earth.... My heart beats with joy at this thought." She was certain that the Lord would not have placed such an intense desire in her heart if He did not want to fulfill it. "When I'm up in heaven, how many graces I will beg

---

[83] St. Thérèse of Lisieux, Letters 253, 220, and 258, in *Letters*, vol. 2, pp. 1140, 1059, and 1154.
[84] St. Thérèse of Lisieux, Letter 254, in *Letters*, vol. 2, p. 1142.

for you.... I'll torment God so much that my importunity will force Him to grant my desires."[85] Thérèse was convinced that graces she herself had received were due to the prayers of someone "who begged them from God for me, and whom I shall know only in heaven." There, "all the elect will discover that they owe to each other the graces that merited the crown for them."[86] When the chaplain told Thérèse that soon she would be leaving her sisters in death, she responded that rather than leaving them, in fact, she would be far closer to them. She also promised that in heaven she would obtain many favors for those who had helped her. "You won't even be able to make use of them all, there will be so many to enjoy." After her sister Pauline (Mother Mary Agnes) showed her a special kindness, Thérèse promised that in heaven she would reward her for her tender care.[87] How many of us have experienced this grace of answered petitions when we have prayed to saints and to our deceased loved ones and begged for their loving help.

Thérèse enjoyed a special closeness with Fr. Maurice Bellière, for whom she had promised to pray. Convinced that the Lord had given them to one another as brother and sister so that together they could attain the salvation of many others, Thérèse told him that only in heaven would he know how very dear he is to her heart: "Our union, far from being broken, will become more intimate."[88] As Thérèse neared her death, she wrote to him that she was not afraid to die, even though she was very imperfect, for the Lord Himself, in His infinite mercy, would prepare her.

---

[85] St. Thérèse of Lisieux, *Her Last Conversations*, pp. 102, 48.

[86] Ibid., p. 100.

[87] Ibid., pp. 74, 81, 193.

[88] St. Thérèse of Lisieux, Letter 22, in *Letters*, vol. 2, pp. 1059, 1060.

She promised Fr. Bellière that, after her death, she would always be near him, helping him in his every need, and making it easier for him to dwell even now in heaven with her.[89] Thérèse surely would assure us that the Lord wants each of us to experience this same precious grace: the constant help and closeness of our deceased loved ones and of all the blessed in heaven.

The Saints' Compassion for Us
The saints share not only in the Lord's love for every one of us but also in His mercy toward us. Even when our sins and faults are revealed to them, the blessed are filled with only love for us. Nothing about our sins shocks them, for they, too, struggled with weakness and temptation. When Fr. Bellière feared that, in heaven, Thérèse would clearly see all his sins and have less regard for him, Thérèse responded that the opposite is true. Assuring him that the blessed in heaven have tremendous compassion on us in our weakness, she wrote, "They remember, being weak and mortal like us, they committed the same faults." This is why "their fraternal tenderness becomes greater,"[90] for they share in the love of the Lord, who completely "forgets" our sins.[91]

Thérèse was convinced that the merciful love of the Lord Jesus is too little known and that more of us would rejoice in His mercy if we would humbly recognize our nothingness without Him.[92] "My way is all confidence and love. I do not understand souls who fear a Friend so tender."[93] Aware of her weakness and of the Lord's compassion for her, Thérèse assures us that without

[89] St. Thérèse of Lisieux, Letter 261, in *Letters*, vol. 2, p. 1164.
[90] St. Thérèse of Lisieux, Letter 263, in *Letters*, vol. 2, p. 1173.
[91] St. Thérèse of Lisieux, Letter 261, in *Letters*, vol. 2, p. 1164.
[92] St. Thérèse of Lisieux, Letter 226, in *Letters*, vol. 2, p. 1094.
[93] St. Thérèse of Lisieux, Letter 226, in *Letters*, vol. 2, p. 1093.

His mercy, she herself would have been a great sinner: "Jesus has forgiven me more than St. Mary Magdalene since He forgave me in advance by preventing me from falling."[94] In heaven we will not feel shame that others know our sins, for the blessed share in the Lord's own tender compassion for us.[95]

Here on earth, no relationship, no family, is without its wounds. Along with many joys, we can experience misunderstandings, arguments, separation, heartbreaking divisions. In heaven, however, all these wounds will be healed, and every relationship, every family, will be made wonderfully whole. "Love is patient; love is kind;... it is not ... resentful; it does not rejoice in wrongdoing.... Love never ends" (1 Cor. 13:4–6, 8). In an exquisite homily, an early Christian bishop and saint describes the perfect love that now binds St. Stephen with St. Paul, who had participated in Stephen's murder. Stephen entered heaven first, and Paul followed him, "helped by the prayer of Stephen. This, surely, is the true life ... a life in which Paul feels no shame because of Stephen's death, and Stephen delights in Paul's companionship, for love fills them both with joy."[96]

This same forgiving love fills the souls of everyone in heaven, including babies who were aborted, and who, we may hope and trust, are in heaven through the merciful love of the Trinity. The *Catechism of the Catholic Church* reminds us that the Divine Persons of the Trinity, who have created the sacrament of Baptism, through which we receive sanctifying grace, are not bound by the sacraments They have created. The Lord Jesus'

[94] St. Thérèse of Lisieux, *Story of a Soul*, p. 83.
[95] St. Thérèse of Lisieux, Letter 263, in *Letters*, vol. 2, p. 1173.
[96] St. Fulgentius of Ruspe, Sermon 3, Office of Readings for the feast of St. Stephen, in *Liturgy of the Hours*, vol. 1 (New York: Catholic Book Publishing, 1975), p. 1257.

own tenderness toward children and His command "Let the little children come to me" (Matt. 19:14; Luke 18:16) allows us "to hope that there is a way of salvation for children who have died without Baptism" (CCC 1257, 1261). Parents responsible for the abortion of their babies can and should beg forgiveness from their babies, who surely bestow that forgiveness on their parents with all the power of their love.

"All who hate a brother or sister are murderers," and "murderers do not have eternal life abiding in them" (1 John 3:15). It is impossible for those in heaven to bear a grudge against anyone who has ever hurt them. If we ourselves bear wounds within us caused by those who have died, let us know that they now beg our forgiveness. If we are grieving a wrong we have done to loved ones who have died, let us be consoled that they have completely forgiven us and do not even recall our offense. Such is the perfect, compassionate love that fills all the blessed in heaven, a love that we pray may fill each of us even now.

Our Closeness in Heaven to Those We Have Loved on Earth

Our homecoming to heaven will fill all the angels and saints with "a jubilation, a gladness," but, in a special way, those we have loved on earth will receive us into their midst with particular joy, delighting to share forever the love that had bound us together on earth.[97] St. Cyprian's beautiful words give special gladness to our souls: "A great number of our dear ones there await us, a dense throng longs for us. How great a joy both for them and for us to come into their sight and embrace!"[98] Cyprian urges us to

---

[97] St. Catherine of Siena, *The Dialogue*, 41, p. 83.
[98] St. Cyprian, *On Mortality* 26.

be eager to join our loved ones, for we will find again in heaven, and far more wonderfully, all the joys we had together on earth, including blessings we wanted but never had.

As we have seen, St. Thérèse dearly loved her family. As she prepared for her death, the thought of being with all of them again in heaven filled her with delight. She wrote to her beloved sister Céline, "The joys of our childhood, the Sunday evenings, the intimate chats ... all this will be restored to us forever!"[99] Thérèse also wrote to Fr. Roulland, thanking him for praying for her deceased parents and promising to pray, both on earth and in heaven, for his living parents: "And when their course here below is ended, I shall come to get them in your name and introduce them to heaven. How sweet will be the family life we shall enjoy throughout eternity!"[100]

"I shall come to get them." What consoling words! Surely Thérèse's promise is echoed by our deceased loved ones who will be very near to us at our death, strengthening us and gently bringing us home. Every trial we endured on earth will be blessed by the joy of being reunited with our families and loved ones forever. Although Thérèse herself enjoyed a beautiful family life, as we have seen, it was not without its sorrows. Four of her little siblings died as babies, her mother died when Thérèse was very young, and her father suffered from sickness and dementia. And yet these very trials made her all the more anxious to be with her beloved family again. Thérèse was utterly confident that, in heaven, she would be reunited with her beloved mom and dad and siblings, "never to leave each other. There we shall

[99] St. Thérèse of Lisieux, Letter 130, in *Letters*, vol. 2, p. 732.
[100] St. Thérèse of Lisieux, Letter 226, in *Letters*, vol. 2, p. 1095.

taste family joys eternally."[101] What a profound comfort Thérèse's words are to every one of us: we shall enjoy heaven not simply as individuals but also and especially as members of the beautiful families that the Trinity intended and created for us from all eternity, families healed of all wounds, perfectly united, and overflowing with intimate love.

Thérèse realized that those who love one another want to be together, physically close to each other, and she assures us that this great joy is granted to us in heaven. The Trinity, who joined us to our loved ones on earth, will unite us in heaven not only in a spiritual closeness but also in a true physical closeness. "You will take your place at my side."[102] "Never, never will Jesus separate us."[103] Thérèse made these lovely promises to her dear sister Céline. There is a wonderful simplicity in Thérèse's assumption that we will be physically close in heaven to those we love, and she draws this conclusion by making her own these beautiful words of the Lord: "Father, I desire that those also whom you have given me, may be with me where I am" (John 17:24).

We cannot help wondering how we will communicate in heaven with one another, especially with those to whom we have been close on earth. A single glance of love will be enough, Thérèse tells us, a glance through which we will communicate from the depths of our souls all that we are, with nothing held back and everything shared. Thérèse wrote to her sister Léonie that in heaven they would completely understand one another: "In my look you will see all I would like to say to you." Thérèse also promised her dear aunt Céline Guérin that in heaven she would be able to tell her many

---

[101] St. Thérèse of Lisieux, Letter 148, in *Letters*, vol. 2, p. 816.

[102] St. Thérèse of Lisieux, *Her Last Conversations*, p. 217.

[103] St. Thérèse of Lisieux., Letter 167, in *Letters*, vol. 2, p. 871.

things that are impossible to express in words on earth.[104] What joy it will be in heaven to know that all that we think and feel will be communicated to our loved ones with no possibility of misunderstanding. St. Catherine of Siena assures us that in heaven no hiding of ourselves, no selfishness, exists, but "only a familial charity in which each one shares in the good of the other." Our closeness to loved ones on earth thus enables us to experience "through charity in this life what we shall see face to face in the next."[105]

When we join the company of saints and angels, we bring with us the tremendous virtue of charity, which fills us on earth with love for the Trinity and for one another. Forever we will love with the very same degree of charity with which we enter heaven. It is this charity that binds us to the blessed and most especially to those we have dearly loved on earth, causing us to "rejoice in each other's reward" and to exult in the Trinity "with jubilation and mirth."[106]

We also will have the great joy of meeting the myriads of angels who have been close to us on earth, and with whom we have worshipped the Trinity, particularly in the Eucharistic celebration: "The multitude of angels extols Your majesty, and we are united with them in exultant adoration."[107] The beautiful "Cherubic Hymn" of the Divine Liturgy of St. John Chrysostom cries out, "Let us, who mystically represent the cherubim, and sing the thrice-holy hymn to the life-creating Trinity, now set aside all earthly cares,

---

[104] St. Thérèse of Lisieux, *Her Last Conversations*, p. 105; Letters 163 and 152, in *Letters*, vol. 2, pp. 853, 833.

[105] St. Catherine of Siena, Letter DT I, in *The Letters of Catherine of Siena*, vol. 2, trans. Suzanne Noffke, O.P. (Tempe, AZ: Center for Medieval and Renaissance Texts and Studies, 2001), p. 53.

[106] St. Catherine of Siena, *The Dialogue* 41, 148, pp. 83, 313.

[107] Preface for the feast of the Guardian Angels, The Liturgy Archive, http://www.liturgies.net/saints/guardianangels/mass.htm.

that we may receive the King of All, invisibly escorted by angelic hosts."[108] How many times we have joined our praise to that of the angels during the Preface of the Mass: "With the choirs of angels, with all the heavenly host, we proclaim Your glory and join in their unending hymn of praise."[109] How often we have prayed to St. Michael the Archangel, asking him to "be our protection" against "the snares of the devil."

What joy it will be also to meet the heavenly spirits who have served, guided, and protected us here on earth! We will realize with profound gratitude the countless times the angels have saved us from harm: "The angel of the LORD encamps round about those who fear him, and delivers them" (Ps. 34:7). The Lord Himself speaks of our guardian angels, whom we surely will greet with grateful joy in heaven: "Do not despise one of these little ones; . . . their angels continually see the face of my Father in heaven" (Matt. 18:10). St. Gregory of Nazianzus assures us that the angels, who faithfully love and help us now and whose invisible worship of the Trinity we join in our celebration of the Mass here on earth, eagerly await our homecoming. It is these angels who will come to carry us gently home to heaven's joy.[110]

"He will command his angels concerning you to guard you in all your ways" (Ps. 91:11). These words, St. Bernard tells us, should fill us with great love for the angels as well as a tender devotion to them and great confidence in them. How faithfully the angels serve us, and how powerfully they protect us! We owe

---

[108] "The Divine Liturgy: The Great Entrance," Byzantine Catholic Archeparchy of Pittsburgh, https://mci.archpitt.org/liturgy/Divine_Liturgy_Great_Entrance.html.

[109] Preface I of Sundays in Ordinary Time, Oremus, http://www.oremus.org/liturgy/tcw/ep-may99/prefaces.html#p19.

[110] St. Gregory of Nazianzus, *Oration 43: On St. Basil* 79.

so much to them: not only our love and affection, but also our constant gratitude. What joy it should give us to realize that, just as they serve as our guardians here on earth, they will be our "coheirs" forever in heaven.[111]

There, in heaven's ecstasy, we will all gladly share in one another's joy, with each one of us reflecting in an absolutely unique way a precious facet of the Lord's love. Some will shine because of their humility; others will be radiant because of their patience or contemplation or teaching. Yet at the heart of all these gifts will be charity, glowing wondrously in each one.[112] It is this beautiful virtue that shares in the Trinity's self-giving love and that joins all the angels and saints to one another in a union that is far more intimate than we could now imagine.

The most profound heavenly closeness will bind together those who, even as they were united on earth by the intimate bonds of family, marriage, or friendship, became "one heart and soul" (Acts 4:32) through their mutual and ardent love for the Lord. For this very reason, St. Bernard urges us now to "long for those who are longing for us," to "hasten to those who are waiting for us."[113] Our loved ones in heaven are yearning for us; they are eagerly anticipating our coming home! As St. Catherine of Siena assures us, our closeness to one another in heaven will be immeasurably deeper and sweeter than any bond of love that may have been ours on earth. Indeed, we will enjoy forever an utterly

---

[111] St. Bernard of Clairvaux, *Sermon 12 on Psalm 91* 3, 6–8, Office of Readings for the feast of the Guardian Angels, in *Liturgy of the Hours*, vol. 4, p. 1454.

[112] St. Catherine of Siena, *The Dialogue* 148, pp. 312, 313.

[113] St. Bernard of Clairvaux, *Sermon 2*, Office of Readings for the solemnity of All Saints, The Liturgy Archive, http://www.liturgies.net/saints/allsaints/officeofreadings.htm.

unique, intimate, and "special kind of sharing" with those whom we loved with a "special love" on earth, and through which we helped one another grow in grace and virtue. Far from losing the profound love we had for one another on earth, we will love one another "even more closely and fully," adding our unique, profound love to the tender communion among us all.[114]

Dante ends his *Paradiso* with a vision in which everything that was scattered and divided in the universe is finally united, bound together by love. In heaven, with every wound and deprivation healed, we will rush to receive one another's tender embrace: families and relatives, loved ones and friends. All that we thought we had lost through death, every blessing we desired on earth but never attained, is restored and bestowed on us a thousand times over in heaven.[115] With our hearts filled to overflowing with the Trinity's ecstatic, self-giving love, we will enjoy forever the closeness of one another in the marvelous Communion of Saints.

---

[114] St. Catherine of Siena, *The Dialogue* 41, p. 83.

[115] St. Ambrose, *On the Death of Emperor Theodosius* 40, in *Funeral Orations by Saint Gregory Nazianzen and Saint Ambrose*, trans. Roy J. Deferrari (New York: Fathers of the Church, 1953), p. 325.

3

The Joy of Our Resurrection

"I am the resurrection and the life. Those who believe in me, even though they die, will live" (John 11:25). At the end of time, the Blessed Trinity will complete the great work begun in us when we were baptized. Redeemed by Jesus' death, we look forward to sharing in His glorious Resurrection. "In my flesh I shall see God" (Job 19:26). In our very own bodies, we shall delight in the Blessed Trinity, enjoy the company of the angels and saints, and gaze into the eyes of our loved ones. We will delight in their laughter, hold their dear hands, and feel their warm embrace once again. What longing should fill our hearts as we proclaim every Sunday in the Nicene Creed, "I *look forward* to the resurrection of the body."

Our Glorious Resurrection in Jesus

We would have been created in vain if we had been unable to obtain the purpose for which the Trinity destined us: to enjoy, not only in our souls but also in our very own bodies, the wonders of the Trinity and the closeness of our loved ones in heaven. By the loving design of the Trinity, the soul is a spiritual substance that is naturally immortal and has its full perfection in being united to the body.[116] The death to which sin has made us subject (Rom. 6:23) means the separation of our souls from our bodies (CCC 1005). Through infinite love, however, the Trinity have bestowed on us the unmerited gift of immortal life for our bodies also, gained for us through the death and Resurrection of the Lord Jesus. How magnificent our joy will be, forever delighting in the wonders of heaven with every part of us, soul and body!

Although death will separate our souls from our bodies, our resurrection in Jesus means that one day we shall know the joy of having our bodies forever reunited with our souls. As St. Augustine assures us, our risen bodies will be the same bodies we have now—anything else would not be resurrection—but our bodies will be wondrously transformed. Truly physical, they will share in the glory of the Lord's risen body and will be forever immortal and incorruptible, utterly permeated with the Spirit of Life (1 Cor. 15:42–44).[117] Nothing natural can cause this glorious transformation of our bodies at the resurrection; it is a sheer miracle of the Trinity's love for us, freely given to us in and through the Lord's Resurrection.

"As all die in Adam, so all will be made alive in Christ" (1 Cor. 15:22). The Resurrection of the Lord Jesus is the great cause of *our* resurrection. He who is life itself gave His body to be tortured and finally devoured by the forces of death caused by our sin (Rom. 5:12; 1 Cor. 15:21). Through love alone, He submitted to the most excruciating suffering and death for our sake (Eph. 5:25). The same love with which the Lord died for us,

---

[116] St. Thomas Aquinas, *Summa Theologiae*, Supp. 75.1.4.
[117] St. Augustine, *City of God* 13.20.

however, was the power by which He utterly vanquished death, our great enemy (1 Cor. 15:26). From within death itself, and by the very power of His love, He stripped death of its power to destroy us. The Church in her Liturgy cries out: "What a great work of charity! Death itself died when Life was slain on the tree."[118]

The Lord rose from the dead, with His human body completely transformed into a glorious, immortal body, freed from the limitations of time and space and able to live within us, most intimately in the Eucharist. No longer subject to suffering or death, the Lord's risen body is permeated with the Holy Spirit's glory, pervaded with unending, risen, indestructible life, which we are destined to share: "If the Spirit of him who raised Jesus from the dead dwells in you, he who raised Christ from the dead will give life to your mortal bodies also" (Rom. 8:11).

Even as His body lay in the grave, the Lord extended His life-giving power to the souls of those who had lived in love before Him. We have noted already an exquisite homily by an early Christian writer who pictures the Lord after His death descending to the place of the dead, seeking out our first parents, and bidding them, in Him, to rise from the dead: "You are in me and I am in you; together we form only one person and we cannot be separated."[119] When we are united intimately to the Lord through sanctifying grace, the power of the Lord's Resurrection fills us also (Col. 2:12; Rom. 6:4).

[118] Feast of the Exaltation of the Holy Cross, First Antiphon of Evening Prayer I, The Liturgy Archive, http://www.liturgies.net/saints/holycross/eveningprayer2.htm.
[119] "An Ancient Homily on Holy Saturday."

Our Resurrection at the End of Time

Church Fathers such as St. Gregory of Nazianzus never tired of proclaiming the Lord's Resurrection,[120] because, as St. Maximus assures us, with His Resurrection, "the hope of resurrection has everywhere been awakened."[121] Our death has been conquered by the Risen Lord of life. Now we, too, can look forward to our resurrection in Him.

We cannot help wondering, however, when this resurrection will occur. In response, the Lord tells us that His Father's will is that He raise up "on the last day" all that the Father has given Him (John 6:39). These words, "on the last day," are repeated in John 6:40, 44, and 54. Scripture thus assures us that our resurrection will occur at the end of time, when the Lord Jesus will completely manifest to us His magnificence at His Second Coming in glory, when the Last Judgment will occur (1 Thess. 4:16–18; Matt. 25:31–36). It is wonderfully fitting that our resurrection in Jesus will occur at the end of time, when, as the Lord's one Mystical Body, we will rise together,[122] in communion with the Lord and with one another, and when everything will be a wondrous "now."[123]

Before the resurrection, the blessed in heaven are perfectly happy because the Divine Persons of the Trinity are the fulfillment of our every longing. Nevertheless, they still desire to enjoy

---

[120] St. Gregory of Nazianzus, "On the Holy Pasch, Second Sermon," in M. F. Toal, trans. and ed., *The Sunday Sermons of the Great Fathers*, vol 2. (San Francisco: Ignatius Press, 1996), p. 246.

[121] St. Maximus, "On the Lord's Resurrection and the Prayer of the Good Thief," in Toal, *Sunday Sermons*, vol. 2, p. 239.

[122] St. Thomas Aquinas, *Summa Theologiae*, Supp. 77.1.

[123] St. Augustine, *Confessions* 11.11.

The Joy of Our Resurrection

the Trinity in a such a way that this joy overflows into their bodies,[124] since the union of our bodies and souls is the perfect state intended for us by the Trinity.[125] St. Augustine comments that, although the souls of the blessed in heaven are perfectly happy in the presence of the Trinity, they cannot help looking forward "with patient longing" to the resurrection of their bodies.[126] At the resurrection, therefore, our souls' delight in the Trinity will overflow into our bodies,[127] and our bodies will attain their full and glorious perfection, adding a certain lovely "charm" to our heavenly happiness.[128]

St. Gregory of Nyssa recounts a wonderful conversation he had with his sister, St. Macrina, about this beautiful mystery that we human beings are, composed intimately of soul and body. Our souls know and love every particle of matter that forms our bodies, because the Trinity created our souls to be the life principle of our unique bodies. At our death, our souls are separated from our bodies, but, in a mysterious way, our souls continue to be present to every particle of our bodies, regardless of where that matter is scattered. Sts. Gregory and Macrina contemplated how our souls know their own bodies even after thousands of years, because there is a certain "principle of identity" that endures in each particle of our bodies, marking them as belonging to our bodies and to no one else's.[129]

---

124 St. Thomas Aquinas, *Summa Theologiae* I-II.4.5, ad. 4, 5.
125 Ibid., Supp. 93.1.
126 St. Augustine, *City of God* 13.20.
127 St. Catherine of Siena, *The Dialogue* 42, 41.
128 St. Thomas Aquinas, *Summa Theologiae* I-II.4.6, ad. 1.
129 St. Gregory of Nyssa, *On the Soul and Resurrection*, trans. Catharine Roth (Crestwood, NY: St. Vladimir's Seminary Press, 1993), p. 69.

Surely this is a key reason why Catholic cemeteries are consecrated as holy ground and why we so honor and adorn the burial places of our loved ones. Their bodies, once living temples of the Holy Spirit (1 Cor. 6:19), are buried there, not their souls. And yet their souls, as spiritual substances, are intimately present to their bodies, as they joyfully await being united with their transformed bodies at the resurrection. This is why, even though *they* are not in the grave, we can sense the closeness of our loved ones at the gravesites of their bodies.

Sts. Gregory and Macrina marveled at how, at the end of time, our souls will draw to themselves the matter that formed our bodies here on earth, since our souls will not then be contained by matter and will be able to go immediately wherever they desire. This reunion of our souls with the same bodies we had on earth—but now gloriously transformed in the Risen Jesus—is true resurrection. Anything else would be the creation of a different person. Sts. Gregory and Macrina tell us that the wondrous power of the Trinity not only gives back to us what was dissolved in our bodies through death, but also adds other amazing gifts through which our bodies become even more beautiful, glorious, and complete. Our risen bodies thus will be made absolutely radiant with "incorruptibility, glory, honor, power, and every kind of perfection."[130]

There is one magnificent exception for us human beings as we look forward to our resurrection at the end of time: our Blessed Mother. We are inspired and tenderly helped by the presence and love of her whose assumption, soul and body, into heaven has already occurred, giving us a glimpse of our own risen destiny at the end of time. In a beautiful homily on our Blessed Mother's

---

[130] Ibid., pp. 67, 118.

The Joy of Our Resurrection

Dormition, or "falling asleep" in death, St. Andrew of Crete sings out in praise: Because her Child "put corruption to flight," her tomb "did not admit of corruption—for it has no claim on holy things.... Let us sing to the Mother of God.... This is *our* frame that we celebrate."[131]

Our Blessed Mother's death was an indescribably sweet "falling asleep" in her Son, who conquered death by His Resurrection.[132] He whose sacred body was formed from hers, would not let His Mother's precious body taste corruption. As Eastern Fathers such as St. John Damascene stress, she did undergo death, in union with her Son, who submitted Himself to our death, but death could not hold her. Jesus, her Son and Lord, completely conquered the power of death within her by the strength of His Resurrection.[133] He raised His dear Mother from death to heaven's heights, transforming her dead body into a magnificent risen body after her death. She, whom the Lord gave us to be our Mother also (John 19:27), has shown us in her Assumption into heaven a unique and remarkable foretaste of the joy of our resurrection at the end of time (CCC 966).

The Marvelous Qualities of Our Risen Bodies

What tremendous delight it will bring us in heaven to glorify the Trinity for the beauty of our risen bodies, and for the exquisite joy

---

[131] St. Andrew of Crete, "On the Dormition of the Mother of God," Homily 1, in *On the Dormition of Mary: Early Patristic Homilies*, trans. Brian E. Daley, S.J. (Crestwood, NY: St. Vladimir's Seminary Press, 1998), pp. 110, 104, 114.

[132] St. Andrew of Crete, "On the Dormition of the Mother of God," Homily 2, in *On the Dormition of Mary*, pp. 119, 121.

[133] St. John Damascene, "On the Dormition," Homily 1, in *On the Dormition of Mary*, pp.194–198.

of seeing and embracing our loved ones in their resplendent risen bodies! St. Augustine contemplates the mystery of our having in heaven risen bodies that are truly physical but also "spiritual" (1 Cor. 15:44), permeated with the Holy Spirit and freed from every kind of imperfection.[134] Completely subject to our souls, they will have no more struggles, pain, or weaknesses of any kind. Our risen bodies will be glorious, full of beauty and grace, with everything in us endlessly praising the Trinity. Each person's unique glorified body will reflect the goodness of his or her life[135] and will share in absolutely wonderful ways in the glory of the Lord's risen body.

"There shall be no more death" (see Rev. 21:4). The first tremendous gift of the Trinity that will fill our risen bodies will be that of immortality: "What is sown is perishable, what is raised is imperishable.... This mortal body must put on immortality" (1 Cor. 15:42–53).[136] By nature, our spiritual souls, not our physical bodies, are immortal, unable to die. As we have seen, however, at our resurrection, the Trinity will transform our mortal bodies into glorious risen bodies that also will be incapable of dying. These bodies will share in the immortality of the Lord's risen body, and reflect the radiant glory of our immortal souls.[137]

How tremendous will be our joy never again to grieve the death of our loved ones, nor to fear the event or circumstances of our own death! "He will wipe every tear from their eyes.... Mourning and crying and pain will be no more" (Rev. 21:4). Filled with gratitude, we will rejoice forever with St. Paul and all the saints over the destruction of death by the power of the Lord's

---

[134] St. Augustine, *City of God* 22.21, 24.
[135] St. Catherine of Siena, *The Dialogue* 42, p. 86.
[136] St. Thomas Aquinas, *Summa Theologiae*, Supp. 82.1.
[137] St. Catherine of Siena, *The Dialogue* 42, p. 85.

The Joy of Our Resurrection

Resurrection in us: "Where, O death, is your victory? Where, O death, is your sting?" (1 Cor. 15:55).

This amazing gift of immortality would be in vain without the accompanying gift of impassibility, our risen body's inability to suffer sickness, pain, or weakness ever again: "Pain will be no more" (Rev. 21:4). Our risen bodies and the risen bodies of our loved ones will be wondrously youthful, vigorous, and at the perfect age, regardless of how old or young we were when we died. The Lord rose from the dead when He was in His early thirties, at the very prime of human life. Because our resurrection shares in His, it is fitting that we, too, will rise at the age of our fullest vigor. Radiant with a loveliness we could never have imagined on earth, our risen bodies will have the perfect dimensions that they attained or would have attained in the prime of our lives.[138]

At the resurrection, our bodies thus will be raised and transformed, completely whole and full of glowing good health. Any illness, weakness, or defect, physical, mental, or emotional, that we or our loved ones may have suffered on earth will be magnificently healed. Since the Trinity created each of us to be perfectly whole as a man or as a woman (Gen. 1:27; 5:2; Mark 10:6; Matt. 19:4), our risen bodies will be made absolutely perfect in every possible way. Healed of all deprivations, they will be endowed with every beautiful physical quality and will never suffer from any imperfection again.[139]

St. Augustine consoles us tremendously when he tells us that those who died at a very young age, or while still in the womb, will receive at the resurrection all that their young bodies were

---

[138] St. Augustine, *City of God* 22.15, 16, 20.
[139] St. Thomas Aquinas, *Summa Theologiae*, Supp. 81.1.

lacking and will rise at the perfect age of maturity. As a miraculous gift of the Trinity, they will receive all the matter that would have belonged to their bodies if they had reached the perfect age on earth, and they will attain "to maturity, to the measure of the full stature of Christ" (Eph. 4:13), enjoying forever the gifts of wonderful health and vigor.[140] What delight it will bring us to see all of our loved ones, regardless of how young or old they were when they died, brimming with the youthful energy of unending life!

St. Thérèse makes a beautiful comment that little ones who died either in the womb or after birth, including the Holy Innocents, surely will not be children in heaven, for everyone will be brought to perfect maturity (Eph. 4:13). Nevertheless, they will always have, in a very unique way, the "indefinable charms" of childhood.[141] On the other hand, those who died in old age will have our lasting respect for their wisdom gained through their many years on earth, but they, too, will be young forever.[142]

Our risen bodies also will have the wonderful quality of agility, entailing great power and ease of movement: "They shall run and not be weary, they shall walk and not be faint" (Isa. 40:31). St. Paul promises us that although our bodies are now "sown in weakness," they shall be raised in power (1 Cor. 15:43). We will have the gift of agility in our glorified souls, but it will overflow magnificently into our risen bodies.[143] Because our glorified

---

[140] St. Augustine, *City of God* 22.14.
[141] St. Thérèse, *Her Last Conversations*, p. 48. On our hope and trust that unbaptized babies are brought to heaven's joy through the merciful love of the Trinity, see chapter 2, p. 37 of this work and CCC 1257 and 1261.
[142] St. Thomas Aquinas, *Summa Theologiae*, Supp. 81.1, ad. 1.
[143] Ibid., 84.1.

bodies will be truly physical but also supremely "spiritual" (1 Cor. 15:44), permeated with the Holy Spirit, nothing about them will be slow or sluggish. Our glorified bodies will possess a beautiful grace, lightness, and tremendous ease in moving.[144] What an inexpressible joy it will be for us and our loved ones—the little ones who died before they could walk, the older ones who died unable even to move—to enjoy leaping for joy and dancing with abandon in heaven!

Here on earth, our bodies alone are not enough to enable us to travel long distances or to distant places. We can walk only so far without growing weary; we can run only so long without growing weak. Through the beautiful gift of agility, however, our bodies will be able to travel instantly wherever we desire to go, moving quickly and with the greatest ease and pleasure.[145] Running "like sparks through the stubble" (Wisd. 3:7), we will never grow tired or weary. How we shall thrill to see our loved ones who died when they were young, now fully mature, and those who died when they were elderly, now vigorous and youthful, never again to grow old or weak.

We will be able to travel all over the universe, in the presence of the Trinity and in the loving and glorious company of one another. St. Thomas Aquinas tells us that our risen bodies will transcend the boundaries of time and space, and will take us wherever our minds desire to go.[146] What delight it will give us to enjoy, with all of our senses, the intoxicating mysteries of our cosmos! Moving through the entire universe with ease, we will joyfully behold its every wonder. Unceasingly refreshed by

[144] Ibid., 84.1, ad. 2.
[145] Ibid.
[146] Ibid., 84.3, ad. 1.

the loveliness of the magnificent seas, mountains, meadows, flowers, and trees, we will behold also the planets and stars of the universe, in which the Trinity's creative wisdom shines with such great splendor. Most wonderful of all, wherever we go, the Trinity will be intimately present to us.[147]

Another wonderful quality of our risen bodies will be what St. Thomas Aquinas calls the gift of subtlety, the power to pass easily through matter. We see this beautiful characteristic in the Lord's glorified body. Although the doors of the upper room were closed, He suddenly appeared to the apostles, for in His glorious body He could pass effortlessly through the doors (John 20:19).[148] Our risen bodies, though truly physical, will not take up space in the way they do here on earth, nor will they occupy the same space as the glorified body of another person.[149] Rather, the subtlety of our risen bodies is a mystery whose wonder we can appreciate when we think of the countless rays of light that can exist in a single building, or the innumerable perfumed scents that can permeate a single room, or the manifold thoughts that can exist in one mind. So it is with heaven: there will be no crowding, and every person will feel utterly free and unhindered by the presence of countless others.

The gift of clarity, beauty that is radiant and full of light, is still another wondrous characteristic of our risen bodies: "The righteous will shine like the sun in the kingdom of their Father" (Matt. 13:43). Our bodies, "sown in dishonor," will be "raised in glory" (1 Cor. 15:43) and will "shine like the sun" (Matt 13:43). With a glory more luminous than the stars, our risen bodies will

---

147 Ibid., 84.2.
148 Ibid., 83.1.
149 Ibid., 83.4.

glow with magnificent light.[150] A great joy for every one of us will be feasting on this splendor of love and beauty shining from all those in heaven, especially our loved ones. Through grace, the Trinity's glory will illumine our bodies with resplendent light, and the Trinity's love in us will shine as our most beautiful adornment, making us and our loved ones even more gorgeous to behold.

Although our risen bodies will be truly physical, they will never hide or withhold from others what we are feeling or who we truly are. Rather, they will reveal our deepest identities and will wonderfully give to others the gift of our inmost selves. Because each soul will have a greater or lesser brilliance according to its degree of love, everyone's beauty will be absolutely unique (1 Cor. 15:41).[151] Sharing in the glory of the Lord's risen body, the distinctive radiance of our glorified bodies will reflect the love within us, the good that all of us, even those unborn, have spread through our earthly lives, regardless of how brief.

Heaven will thus be full of magnificent colors shining brilliantly from every one of us. This resplendent beauty will not hurt our physical eyesight, but rather, will soothe it, even though the glory of each of us will surpass the splendor of the sun.[152] How tremendous will be our joy to see, with our own eyes, first of all, the indescribable glory of the Lord's risen body, and then the loveliness of Our Blessed Mother, the saints, and especially our dear ones, so beautiful to us on earth and now tremendously more glorious and radiant in heaven.

---

[150] Ibid., 85.1.
[151] Ibid.
[152] Ibid., 85.2, ad. 2.

All of Creation Sharing in
the Glory of Our Resurrection

Not only we but also the entire universe will be magnificently renewed at the end of time: "I am about to create new heavens and a new earth" (Isa. 65:17); "I saw a new heaven and a new earth … prepared as a bride adorned for her husband" (Rev. 21:1–2). St. Augustine comments that the Trinity will recreate the world for a wonderful reason: to be a more beautiful environment for us as we share in the glory of the Risen Lord.[153] St. Thomas Aquinas adds that because our glorified bodies will be glowing with the magnificence of the stars,[154] the Divine Persons, who are loveliness itself, will fill the earth with every kind of luminous beauty on which our souls and glorified senses can feast.[155]

In a special way, magnificent light shining from all of created reality will enthrall us in heaven. We know that everything around us seems to darken with gloom when the skies are gray. After the rain, however, when the sun bursts forth, the whole world seems to awaken with new splendor, glistening with gorgeous sunlight. This experience gives us an intimation of how wondrously all of creation will be illumined by brilliant light, providing a feast for our eyes, the most spiritual and subtle of our senses:[156] "The light of the moon will be like the light of the sun, and the light of the sun will be sevenfold" (Isa. 30:26).

The magnificence of our universe helps us to know and glorify the Trinity, whose infinite beauty we glimpse through savoring the grandeur of created things (Rom. 1:20). "From the greatness

---

[153] St. Augustine, *City of God* 20.16.

[154] St. Thomas Aquinas, *Summa Theologiae*, Supp. 91.4, ad. 4.

[155] Ibid., 91.1.

[156] Ibid., 91.4, ad. 1.

and beauty of created things," their Creator can be seen and known (Wisd. 13:5).[157] In heaven we will not see the Trinity's infinite glory directly with our eyes, but rather with intellectual vision, through union with the Divine Persons in the ecstasy of the Beatific Vision.[158] Our physical eyes will gaze on the Trinity's beauty, however, as an object of indirect vision, reflected most of all in the risen body of the Lord Jesus, then in the glorified bodies of our Mother Mary and of all the blessed, and finally, in a marvelous way, in all of creation.[159]

St. Augustine invites us to meditate on the tremendous beauty even now of the created world around us. The Persons of the Trinity have generously and graciously given us the marvels of the universe as a foretaste of the re-created universe that we will enjoy at the end of time. Even now, there is no way we can adequately laud the power of the sea, the glory of a sunlit sky, or the "miraculous loveliness" of light as it shines in the sun and the stars and is reflected in the moon. No words can fully describe the countless shades of green in the forest, the magnificent variety of flowers, the multitude of animals; the dark shades of the woods, the color and fragrance of flowers; the amazing varieties of birds, with their unique songs and colorful feathers; the numerous creatures of all shapes and sizes; the seas and oceans with their varied beauty of colors. The glories of the sun and the moon, the stars and the planets; the beauty of night turning into day, the marvel of sunlight and cool breezes: these wonders of nature never cease to amaze us.[160]

[157] Ibid., 92.2.
[158] Ibid., 92.2, ad. 7; 92.1, ad. 2.
[159] Ibid., 92.2.
[160] St. Augustine, *City of God* 22.24.

When we gaze on the great beauty contained in our world, we have a glimpse of the joys of the universe that will greet us at the end of time.[161] These magnificent treasures of the cosmos we will be able to savor as soon as we are in heaven. Their present beauty, however, pales in comparison with the wonders we will enjoy when the entire universe will be re-created to reflect the glory of the Lord's Resurrection and to share in the wonder of our resurrection.[162]

So, too, with the exquisite gift of music. How empty our world would be without this precious gift of the Trinity to us! Beautiful music lifts our spirits and brings peace to our souls. The inspired music of the great masters can fill us with jubilation and touch us so deeply that we cry. Surely this is why so many of the psalms urge us to "sing joyfully to the Lord," to praise the Lord with all of our might, with dancing, with trumpets, with lyre and harp (e.g., Psalms 33, 47, 92, 149). St. Paul encourages us to sing hymns and psalms, glorifying the Lord with hearts full of gratitude (Col. 3:16). St. John of the Cross even tells us that intimate union with the Trinity here on earth inspires in us a "song of the soul" whose melody is exceedingly sweet to the Trinity and whose delight is beyond description. The most magnificent melodies on earth, however, cannot compare with the beauty and "incomparably more precious" "new song" that is the music of heaven.[163]

The book of Revelation gives us a wonderful glimpse of this magnificent heavenly singing to the Lord, who is worthy to receive all "glory and honor and power" (Rev. 4:11). How tremendous it will be to share in the exquisite music of the angels and

---

[161] Ibid., 22.21.
[162] Ibid., 91.1.
[163] St. John of the Cross, *The Spiritual Canticle* 39.9–10 , pp. 560–561.

saints praising the Trinity with their enchanting melodies and magnificent "new song" (Rev. 5:9; 15:3). As companions of the angels and saints, we will dance and sing and exult in forming one community of love, with the most magnificent peace, love, and joy reigning within and among us.[164]

What happiness it gives us to meditate on these wonders of heaven, St. Augustine cries out, where everything is good, and where God the Trinity is "all in all." Free of idleness and boredom, we will be enraptured forever by the Divine Persons, who are beauty itself, and by the incomparable glory radiating from the risen body of the Lord Jesus. With our wills fixed on the Trinity's goodness, we will delight in being unable to sin or to use our glorified bodies as instruments of sin.[165] Created by the Trinity as wondrous composites of physical matter and immortal souls, we will rejoice forever in the Trinity's glory reflected in our risen bodies and inflaming the entire universe with its splendor.[166]

---

[164] St. Augustine, *City of God*, 19.13.

[165] Ibid., 22.30.

[166] St. Thomas Aquinas, *Summa Theologiae*, Supp. 91.3.

4

Dying into the Mercy of the Trinity

Blessed are those who "die in the Lord" (Rev. 14:13). Having meditated on the magnificent wonders that await us in heaven, we turn now to consider our only path to heaven's bliss: our death.

Of itself, death is the ultimate tragedy, the loss of everything we hold dear. We naturally fear it and the sufferings that may precede and accompany it. By faith we know that death, our great "enemy" (1 Cor. 15:26), is the result of sin (Rom. 6:23), entailing the separation of our souls from our bodies. We also know by faith, however, that through His infinite love for us, the Lord has gloriously transformed our death. Choosing to suffer the horrors of crucifixion for our sake, Jesus has vanquished our death by His glorious Resurrection and transformed "the curse of death" into our greatest blessing (see CCC 1005–1009). Rather than being the end of all that we hold dear, our death "in the Lord" is now our doorway to the joys of heaven: "To me, living is Christ and dying is gain" (Phil. 1:21).

Dying into the Death of Jesus

By nature, we cannot help fearing death and the trials that may accompany it. Luke describes the anguish in Jesus' human heart as He faced His death with an agony so intense that "his sweat became like great drops of blood falling down on the ground" (Luke 22:44). Luke also recounts how Jesus' anxiety before the terror of His death forced from His lips these precious words: "Father, if you are willing, remove this cup from me; yet, not my will but yours be done" (Luke 22:42). With infinite love for His Father, the Lord made of His death His most tender, salvific act of love for us.

Jesus died our death so that we might be able to die "in" Him a death that leads us to eternal life. "We do not want you to be uninformed ... about those who have fallen asleep, so that you may not grieve as others do who have no hope" (1 Thess. 4:13). St. Paul calls our death a "falling asleep" in the Lord (1 Cor. 15:18). With these beautiful words, he assures us that death "in the Lord" means surrendering ourselves to the tender arms of Jesus, uniting ourselves to His surrender of Himself on the Cross to His Father.

By freely submitting to torture and death for our sake, the Lord Jesus chose to be not the victim of death but rather the One who "trampled" death, the glorious Risen One who granted life to those "in the tombs."[167] Church Fathers wrote with great beauty of the power of the Lord's death to conquer the force of death over us, the members of His Mystical Body. The sufferings endured by the Lord Jesus became the "medicine" that makes us whole. "Such was the tenderness of His love, even for those who put Him to death," that the crucified Lord asked His Father to forgive them. So great was the power of Jesus on His blessed

---

[167] "Christ is risen from the dead! By death He trampled death, and to those in the tombs He granted life!" Troparion of Pascha, Byzantine Catholic Archeparchy of Pittsburgh, https://mci. archpitt.org/liturgy/Troparion of Pascha.html.

Cross that even some of those who had demanded His crucifixion were later prepared to die for Him.[168]

The true Paschal Lamb was slain, but death itself was vanquished by the outpouring of His precious Blood. In a sermon inspired by the Holy Spirit and delivered with great beauty at the Easter Vigil, an early Church Father proclaims the miracle that the Lord accomplished through His sacred death for us: "He filled the abode of the dead with His splendor and roused from sleep those lying there. Now we, too, do not fear death. It has no power over the Resurrection of the Lord!"[169]

With infinite love, Jesus chose to die the most painful death for our sake, so that we could have His strength and love within us as we face our own deaths. We make the Sign of the Cross with the sign of His death, for His death is the source of our life.[170] United to Him, we know that death no longer has any power over us. We can face death with hope, trusting in the Lord, whose grace will uphold us and awaken us to the glorious, unending life of heaven.

Nevertheless, the Lord understands how difficult it is for us to hold back tears as we come to terms with our death or the death of those close to us. In our sorrow, we are consoled by the Lord Himself, who grieved with Martha and wept over the death of His dear friend Lazarus. St. Thomas Aquinas assures us that the Lord chose to suffer the sadness of our human condition in order to comfort us in our grief. How poignant are the words of the Gospel: "Jesus began to weep" (John 11:35). The tears of Jesus,

---

[168] St. Leo the Great, "On the Passion of Our Lord," in Toal, *Sunday Sermons*, pp. 182, 183.
[169] St. Amphilochius of Iconium, "On the Holy Night of the Pasch, the Easter Vigil," in Toal, *Sunday Sermons*, p. 191.
[170] St. Ambrose, *On the Death of His Brother Satyrus* II.46.

who is the "well-spring of compassion," were tears of mercy for us. "We do not have a high priest who is unable to sympathize with our weaknesses" (Heb. 4:15).[171]

St. Augustine writes that after the death of his beloved mother, St. Monica, it was a great comfort to him to let his tears flow freely.[172] Bishop St. Ambrose, who dearly loved both Monica and Augustine, agrees that tears can be a consoling gift when we grieve our impending death, and especially the death of a loved one. With the Trinity's grace, however, we can trust that our tears eventually will give way to our knowing and experiencing through faith that our loved one is still with us, loving and helping us more dearly than ever.[173] Even more, with time, the death of loved ones can deepen our peace and inspire us to look forward to being reunited with them in heaven's joy.[174] St. Ambrose tells us that the death of his beloved brother Satyrus increasingly freed him from any fear of death. Since he was so close to his brother, he trusted that it would be Satyrus himself who would bring him home to heaven.[175] Many of us have experienced this same precious grace. When someone we love dies, we begin to trust ever more dearly that, at our death, our deceased loved ones will be there, tenderly helping us and bringing us home.

Moreover, in whatever trials and sorrows we may face, we can be certain that the Lord, who willingly suffered immeasurably more than all of our own pain, holds us close to His heart and

---

[171] St. Thomas Aquinas. *Commentary on the Gospel of John*, chap. 11, lect. 5, nos. 1535 and 1537; chap. 12, lect. 5, no. 1652.

[172] St. Augustine, *Confessions* 9, 12, 33.

[173] St. Ambrose, *On the Death of His Brother Satyrus* I.6, 77.

[174] St. Ambrose, *On the Death of His Brother Satyrus*, II.137.

[175] Ibid., 43 and 135.

comforts us "with the milk of great consolation."[176] St. Catherine of Siena assures us that the Divine Persons desire only our deepest good, and that absolutely nothing happens to us except by the Trinity's loving permission. Holding this truth deep in our hearts will make everything much more "easy to bear."[177] A superb doctor may prescribe medicines that, although they have unpleasant side effects, will help to bring us to good health. So, too, the Divine Persons allow suffering in our lives not for our destruction but only for our good. If we pray always for the Trinity's loving will to be accomplished in our lives, with peace of soul we will be "content with everything" that the Divine Persons permit for us.

What bliss will be ours in heaven, where, in comparison with the ocean of joy that will engulf us forever, our every suffering, as well as our very lives on earth, will seem like the mere "point of a needle."[178]

The Trinity's Mercy

The death of loved ones teaches us that when the Lord calls us home, we will not be able to trust in our own merits; our only refuge will be the Trinity's tender mercy. Two great Doctors of the Church, St. Thérèse of Lisieux and St. Catherine of Siena,

---

[176] St. Catherine of Siena, *The Dialogue* 151, p. 323.

[177] St. Catherine of Siena, Letter 12, in *Letters*, vol. 1, pp. 61-62; Letter T 264, in *Letters*, vol. 2, p. 481.

[178] St. Catherine of Siena, Letter T 48, in *The Letters of St. Catherine of Siena*, vol. 4, trans. Suzanne Noffke, O.P. (Tempe, AZ: Center for Medieval and Renaissance Texts and Studies, 2008), p. 135; Letter 48, in *Letters*, vol. 1, p. 147; Letter T 264, in *Letters*, vol. 2, p. 480.

urge us to trust in that mercy at every moment of our lives, and especially in the face of illness and death. Thérèse encourages us, first, to love our littleness and weakness, as St. Paul did, so that we may learn to place all of our trust in the Lord. "The little ones will be judged with great gentleness." Thérèse adds that if she herself were to die at a very old age, she would still be the Lord's "little one." "It is written, 'The Lord will rise up to save the gentle and the humble of the earth.' It doesn't say 'to judge,' but 'to save.'"[179]

When Thérèse was only sixteen, the Lord taught her to rejoice in her weaknesses. For Thérèse, this life-changing realization was "a great grace."[180] Eight years later, as she neared her death, she told her sister that even if she had committed the greatest possible sins, she would still place her trust only in the Lord, for all the sins in the world are as nothing compared with the immensity of divine mercy.[181] As she would think of her faults, "with great gentleness and without any sadness," Thérèse would say to herself, "It's so good to feel that one is weak and little" and "I have my weaknesses, but I rejoice in them."[182]

It is the devil who wants us to look only at our sins rather than at the infinite mercy of the Trinity. St. Catherine of Siena encourages us to stand against the devil's "great malice" by crying out, "I trust in the Blood of the Lamb," for our sins can never be greater than the Trinity's mercy. "Even if all the sins that could possibly be committed" were gathered together in one person, St.

---

[179] St. Thérèse of Lisieux, *Her Last Conversations*, p. 199.

[180] St. Thérèse of Lisieux, Letter T 109, in *Letters of St. Thérèse of Lisieux*, vol. I, trans. John Clarke, O.C.D (Washington, D.C.: ICS Publications, 1982), p. 641.

[181] St. Thérèse of Lisieux, *Her Last Conversations*, p. 89.

[182] Ibid., pp. 74, 73.

Dying into the Mercy of the Trinity

Catherine assures us, they would be "like a drop of vinegar in the sea."[183] The Father Himself told Catherine that even those who have spent their entire lives in sin must reach out for the saving power of His mercy. "Because despair displeases me so much, it is my will that they should put their trust in my mercy even at the point of death, after they have spent their life in wickedness."[184] Far more than our sins, it is despair over our sins that truly separates us from the Trinity. The Father's words to Catherine are meant to fill every one of us with hope: "The scorning of my mercy" "offends me more than all" other sins. The despair to which Judas apparently abandoned himself "was a greater insult to my Son than his betrayal had been."[185]

Catherine's life was filled with profound experiences of the Lord's mercy, not only to her but also and especially to the most sinful of persons. Two criminals in Siena being brought to their execution were shouting blasphemies against God. Catherine begged the Lord to have mercy on them through His most precious Blood. She recalled to the Lord His mercy to Peter, to Mary Magdalene, and to the thief on the cross.[186] On the way to their execution, the criminals were converted completely to the Lord. Filled with repentance, they asked for a priest, confessed their sins, and went to their execution with joy and peace.[187] Another man faced the sentence of death for treason. Catherine prayed fervently for him and, at his request, accompanied him to his execution. At his death, Catherine beheld a glorious vision of

---

[183] St. Catherine of Siena, Letter T 314, in *Letters*, vol. 2, p. 486.
[184] St. Catherine of Siena, *The Dialogue* 132. p. 268.
[185] Ibid., 37, p. 79.
[186] Bl. Raymond of Capua, *Life of Catherine* 228, 229, pp. 216, 217.
[187] Ibid., 230, p. 217.

the Lord with His opened side, receiving the man's soul and placing it "all-mercifully into the open hostelry of his side."[188]

Like St. Catherine, St. Thérèse, too, longed to "snatch" even the greatest sinners from the brink of hell. She heard of a great criminal and poured out her soul in prayer for him. After his execution, she read that he had kissed the crucifix the priest had offered him. Thérèse was filled with trust that this poor man's soul received only the mercy of Him who has assured us that "there will be more joy in heaven over one sinner who repents than over ninety-nine righteous persons who need no repentance" (Luke 15:7).[189]

Do we need to fear the prospect of hell, the possibility of our freely hating the Trinity and one another forever? We know by faith that hell is the "state of definitive self-exclusion from communion with God and the blessed" (CCC 1033) and that the demons have chosen hell. But we do not know for certain whether any human being has ever chosen hell. Surely, without the Trinity's grace, we cannot be filled with the love that is the very heart of heaven. We therefore can and must hope and pray that the Trinity's mercy will be victorious in every human heart, including our own.

Great saints such as Catherine of Siena have prayed that no one would ever choose hell, and that the Trinity's love will conquer even the most hardened sinner. Catherine spent her life serving others and praying for their salvation: "I would love that hell should be wiped out; or at least that no soul should ever go there again.... Then my neighbors' souls would all be saved."[190]

---

[188] St. Catherine of Siena, Letter 31 to Raymond of Capua, in *Letters*, vol. 1, pp. 110.

[189] St. Thérèse, *Story of a Soul*, p. 100.

[190] Bl. Raymond of Capua, *Life of Catherine of Siena* 15, p. 14.

Dying into the Mercy of the Trinity

Our part is to pray and trust in the Lord's mercy for ourselves and for everyone else. This virtue of complete trust in the Trinity's mercy does not foster a spirit of presumption and sinning. Rather, it nourishes in our souls an attitude of conversion and total dependence on the grace of the Trinity.

Luke's beautiful account of the repentant thief crucified next to Jesus should fill every one of us with hope and trust (Luke 23:39–43). The thief cried out to the Lord to remember him when He came into His kingdom, and the Lord tenderly responded: "Today you shall be with me in Paradise" (Luke 23:43). This one confession at the very end of his life erased all the sins of his past life. "In that one moment, whatever crimes he had committed, throughout all the years of his life, were now forgiven." The example of this sinner's repentance inspires us to beg for the Lord's saving mercy upon every one of us, regardless of the sins we may have committed.[191] "No one ought to despair," the Father assured St. Catherine of Siena. "My mercy, which you receive in the Blood, is incomparably greater than all the sins that have ever been committed in the world."[192] The Lord Himself cried out in compassion for each of us, "Father, forgive them; for they do not know what they are doing" (Luke 23:34). If the Lord had mercy on His own murderers, how much more will He have mercy on us at our death.[193]

Since our entire life is encompassed by divine mercy, the Lord, who gives us even His most precious Body and Blood as our food does not deprive us of anything we need to die in

---

[191] St. Maximus, "On the Lord's Resurrection," in Toal, *Sunday Sermons*, vol. 2, p. 240.

[192] St. Catherine of Siena, *The Dialogue* 129, p. 260.

[193] St. Maximus, "On the Lord's Resurrection," in Toal, *Sunday Sermons*, vol. 2, p. 240.

peace. Let us pray for the grace truly to repent of our sins and to place all of our hope in the Lord. Trusting in the Lord's mercy will fill us with a confidence that will enable us to prepare for our death and that of our loves with serenity.[194] Then, when we do reach the moment of death, we can trust that the Lord will place us in the tender arms of His Father, who will be for us like a sweet "bed" from which we will awaken to the bliss of eternal life.[195]

Divine Providence Enfolding Our Suffering

As we meditate on the mystery of death, we cannot help thinking of the circumstances of death, especially the possible suffering that we or our loved ones might have to undergo. We have nothing to fear, however, regardless of what the future holds for us. Absolutely everything in our lives, including the time and manner of our death and that of our loved ones, is enfolded in the loving providence of the Blessed Trinity. "Do not worry.... Your heavenly Father knows that you need all these things" (Matt. 6:31–32). The Father told St. Catherine of Siena that those who trust in Him will not be disappointed: "I never fail to give them anything they need. In everything they sweetly experience my providence, tasting in it the milk of divine tenderness, and this is why they do not fear the bitterness of death."[196]

St. Catherine tells us what she herself learned from the Lord: if we make Him our concern, He will take care of everything that concerns us. "Let God's providence watch over you. His eyes are on you continually in your fears. Not a moment passes but he is

---

[194] St. Catherine of Siena, Letter T 314, in *Letters*, vol. 2, p. 486.

[195] St. Catherine of Siena, Letter 29, in *Letters*, vol. 1, p. 103.

[196] St. Catherine of Siena, *The Dialogue*, 151, p. 322.

thinking of your welfare."[197] Even if the Divine Persons permit suffering in our lives or in the lives of our loved ones, it is only to give us and them even greater and sweeter good than we could imagine: "We find God in time of darkness. In bitter things, we find sweetness."[198]

St. John Paul II, who was chosen to share deeply in the Lord's Passion, offers us immense consolation as we contemplate the mystery of suffering that is part and parcel of our death. Jesus Himself prayed before His Passion, "Let this cup pass from me" (Matt. 26:39). Nevertheless, His love for us impelled Him to take upon Himself our sufferings. In doing so, He completely transformed the meaning of our pain. In Him, our trials are a profound share in His redemptive suffering for the salvation of the world,[199] leading us to a bliss that will erase even the memory of any pain of mind, body, or soul that we may have endured.

We find the meaning and purpose of our suffering in Jesus, for the cross always reaches us "together with the resurrection."[200] We pray that our death will be full of peace and without pain. If we are permitted, however, to share in the Lord's agony in some way, large or small, St. Paul assures us that our suffering will bear fruit in unending joy: "This slight momentary affliction is preparing for us an eternal weight of glory beyond all measure" (2 Cor. 4:17).[201]

It is an excruciating trial to endure the pain of our own or a loved one's death at an early age, or under horrific circumstances,

---

[197] Bl. Raymond of Capua, *Life of Catherine* 98, p. 90.
[198] St. Catherine of Siena, Letter T 189, in *Letters*, vol. 2, p. 136.
[199] St. John Paul II, Apostolic Letter *Salvifici Doloris* (February 11, 1984), no. 24.
[200] Ibid., no. 21.
[201] Ibid., no. 22.

or through the evil of others. We naturally rebel at apparently senseless pain and cannot help crying out, perhaps even in rage, "Why? How can a good God let this happen?" St. Thomas Aquinas responds, however, by reminding us of the profound truth that if evil were eliminated from our world, even more tremendous good, such as the very gift of our free will, and especially the outpouring of our love and care for one another in our need, also would disappear from our world.[202]

Jesus endured the most horrible death at the hands of those who cruelly mocked, tortured, and crucified Him. And yet He transformed the horrors of His suffering and death into the precious means of our salvation. How often have we experienced the torrent of others' goodness in response to a seemingly senseless tragedy, horrendous crime, or unimaginable pain? Are we not inspired by those who turn horrific suffering they have witnessed or undergone into heroic acts of love, generosity, and self-giving? Even more, faith tells us that those who have died, regardless of the painful circumstances of their death, would never choose this earthly life over the bliss of heaven. Nor would they ever complain about the sufferings they endured here on earth, sufferings that purified and prepared them for the ecstatic joy of heaven.

St. John Paul II stresses that whatever we or our loved ones are permitted to suffer in union with the Lord, this pain even now "unleashes the mystery of love in us, the unselfish gift of our 'I' on behalf of others." Our own burdens share in the redemptive power of the Lord's suffering for the salvation of the world. No pain or grief, borne in union with the Lord, is wasted or without meaning. When, even in spite of our reluctance to do so, we unite our sufferings to the Lord, our anguish becomes

---

[202] St. Thomas Aquinas, *Summa Theologiae* I.22.2, ad. 2.

a supernatural mystery, its purpose and meaning sharing in the Lord's own salvific love for the world. St. John Paul II invites all who suffer to gather beneath the Cross of Jesus to find *there* the answer to the why of their suffering.[203] In heaven, we will look back on our earthly lives with their blessings and sorrows and cry out to the Trinity with all of our being, "Thank You, Most Blessed Trinity! Absolutely everything was in enfolded in Your loving mercy and providence. *Everything* did indeed "work together for good" (Rom. 8:28).

This in no way means that we should simply submit to any suffering, whether in ourselves or in others, without trying to alleviate it with all our might. When, in union with the Lord, we do all that we can to eliminate suffering in any form, we allow the Lord to continue to act within us to heal the sick, for the Lord is present both in those who suffer and in those who minister to the suffering. The Trinity permit suffering only so that the wondrous mystery of love itself, love that is unselfish and self-giving, may be "unleashed" in our world.[204]

"I was hungry and you gave me food.... Just as you did it to one of the least of these who are members of my family, you did it to me" (Matt. 25:35, 40). Those who care for the sick and the dying, those who minister to others in any kind of need or pain, increase the profound good in the world, for in them the Lord Himself cares for His little ones. So, too, those who suffer unleash in the world tremendous good when they offer their pain to the Lord for the salvation of others. Moreover, they give us the precious gift of drawing forth from us deepened patience, compassion, love, and tender care. This is the profound meaning

---

[203] St. John Paul II, *Salvifici Doloris* 31.

[204] Ibid., nos. 29, 30.

of affliction united to the Lord: those who suffer, especially in union with the Lord, call forth more goodness in the world, and those who minister in any way to those who suffer also release the power of more goodness and love among us. In this double vocation, Jesus has "completely revealed the meaning of our human suffering."[205] If, in spite of our prayers and efforts, the Lord permits sufferings for us or our loved ones, we trust that all we endure will bear magnificent fruit for ourselves and for others, not only now but also in the bliss of heaven. As St. Catherine of Siena reminds us, the Divine Persons "cannot want anything but our good"; treasuring this truth in our souls will help us to be content with all that the Divine Persons permit for us.[206]

Because we are called to alleviate pain whenever we can, we also are called to make our own death and the death of our loved ones as peaceful as possible. The Church encourages us to use palliative care and pain-relieving medication, even if this use would shorten our lives or our loved ones' lives. Our intention is not to bring about death but rather to surround ourselves or our loved ones with as much peace as possible. As we approach death, all normal means of preserving life, such as hydration and nutrition, should be given as long as they can be absorbed and they provide true benefits. We are not required, however, to start or to continue means that are "burdensome, dangerous, extraordinary, or disproportionate to the expected outcome" (CCC 2279, 2278).

What if, in spite of all of our attempts to alleviate our pain or a loved one's pain, we or they experience terrible suffering as death approaches? Are we permitted to cause our own or another's

----

[205] Ibid., no. 30.

[206] St. Catherine of Siena, *The Dialogue* 43, p. 89; Letter T 264, in *Letters*, vol. 2, p. 481.

death in order to be freed of what threatens to be excruciating pain? The answer is an unequivocal no. St. Paul assures us, "You are not your own; you were bought with a price" (see 1 Cor. 6:19–20). Especially for this reason, "we are stewards, not owners, of the life God has entrusted to us. It is not ours to dispose of." Suicide and assisted suicide committed with full knowledge and freedom are gravely sinful (CCC 2280–2281).

It is true that serious psychological disturbances, such as deep depression or irrational fear, reduce the personal responsibility for the grave sin of suicide or assisted suicide. Nevertheless, "an act or omission which, of itself or by intention, causes death in order to eliminate suffering constitutes a murder." This grave sin is an offense against our human dignity and the glory we owe to the Trinity, who created us. Because we are not our own, we are never permitted to cause our death or that of another, even through supposed compassion (CCC 2277, 2282). We thus have a sacred responsibility to obtain psychological, physical, and spiritual help for ourselves or our loved ones who may be tempted to suicide. Yet even if grave psychological disturbances do result in a person's suicide, the Church still hopes in the saving mercy of the Trinity to bring the person to heaven through means unknown to us. We should never despair of the salvation of one who takes his or her own life, but rather enfold the person in our loving prayers (CCC 2283).

If we die in love but our love is not yet perfect, we undergo after our death the loving purification that is called purgatory (CCC 1030). Purgatory itself is a mystery of faith whose exact nature we cannot fathom here on earth. St. Catherine of Siena speaks of the "mercy" of purgatory[207] and assures us that even

---

[207] St. Catherine of Siena, *The Dialogue* 43, p. 89.

in purgatory we find the "gentle immeasurable providence" of the Lord, enfolding us especially through the prayers and Masses offered by others for us.[208] St. Thérèse urges us not to let the thought of purgatory fill us with anxiety but rather to place our trust completely in the Lord. As she neared her death, Thérèse said that she did not know if she would have to undergo the purification of purgatory, but she was "not in the least bit disturbed about it."[209] Certainly the saints encourage us to pray for the grace to be filled with the Trinity's love and forgiveness here on earth so that we will not have to experience purgatory. If we pray to live in love now, with trust in the Trinity's merciful providence, we can face our death with serenity and even joy.[210]

A Death Full of Peace

The best preparation for such a beautiful death is living in the Trinity's self-giving love every day, reaching out to help others, so that, at our death we may hear these precious words of the Lord to us: "Come,... blessed by my Father.... I was hungry and you gave me food.... I was sick and you took care of me" (Matt. 25:34, 35, 36). All of us, even unborn babies, have this irreplaceable purpose: to touch others with the Trinity's tender love in our unique way. We pray that when we come to the moment of death, we may bring with us in spirit our very own "herd of little sheep,"[211] as St. Catherine of Siena calls them, the ones whom our love has drawn more deeply to the Trinity. Even children and

---

[208] Ibid., 148, p. 313.

[209] St. Thérèse, *Her Last Conversations*, p. 56.

[210] St. Catherine of Siena, *The Dialogue* 131, p. 265.

[211] Ibid.

babies, including those unborn, draw others to the Lord through the priceless gift of their lives.

In addition, living and dying in peace requires that, from our heart, we repent of and ask forgiveness for having hurt others, forgiving every grievance or sin committed against us.[212] It might not be possible for us, in person, to ask forgiveness from those we have hurt or to offer forgiveness to those who have hurt us, but it is crucial that we cherish forgiveness in our hearts. In heaven, where only love reigns, no one will hold grudges or recall the sins of others because we will be too full of gratitude to the Lord for His forgiveness of our own sins. As St. Augustine beautifully comments, humbly we will be mindful only of our own sins so that we may all the more joyfully sing of the Lord's steadfast love forever (Ps. 89:1).[213]

The Church encourages us to use whatever means are available to us, medical, psychological, and spiritual, to help us and our loved ones die in the peace and comfort of the Lord. In a special way, the Church offers us tremendous spiritual resources to strengthen us and to heal us spiritually, emotionally, and even physically and to enfold us in the Lord's own peace. Just as Baptism, Confirmation, and the Eucharist form a unity at the very beginning of our Christian lives, the sacraments of the Anointing of the Sick, Reconciliation, and the Eucharist complete our earthly pilgrimage (CCC 1525). Let us not wait until the last moment to make use of the tremendous power available to us and to our loved ones in these precious gifts of the Trinity to us.

The graces of the sacrament of the Anointing of the Sick unite us to the saving power of the Lord's suffering, death, and

---

[212] Bl. Raymond of Capua, *Life of Catherine*, 364, p. 338.
[213] St. Augustine, *City of God* 22.30.

Resurrection, filling us with His comfort, courage, and even physical healing, if this is the Trinity's will for us (CCC 1511–1523). The sacrament of Reconciliation gives us the invaluable means of confessing and truly repenting of all of our sins and of asking for and receiving the Lord's forgiveness. This beautiful sacrament frees us from spiritual burdens that imprison our souls and floods us with the Lord's peace and profound inner healing (CCC 1468). Finally, receiving the Lord's precious Body and Blood in the Eucharist inundates our souls with His own heavenly consolation and sweetness, inspiring our hearts to sing with the psalmist, "Taste and see that the LORD is good" (Ps. 34:8; CCC 1326, 1392, 1402, 1524).

If we are blessed with the sacred privilege of being with someone who is dying, especially a loved one, let us gently pray for and with him or her, particularly to St. Joseph, patron of the dying, and especially for freedom from all anxiety and fear. Saints such as Catherine of Siena show us that demonic attacks can be particularly strong at the bedside of the dying.[214] The Church's prayer to St. Michael the Archangel reminds us that demons constantly "roam through the world, seeking the ruin of souls," especially the souls of the dying. In union with the whole Church, let us use the Lord's command for demons attacking us or our loved ones with fear, anxiety, or despair, to be gone from us and from them in the name of the Lord Jesus (Mark 1:25; 5:8). Some of us may know those who have prayed this command for themselves or with their dying loved ones and who can attest to the power of the Lord in this way to bring serenity to the dying. The aid of an excellent, faith-filled hospice program also can be a great help to the dying and to those who care for them.

---

[214] Bl. Raymond of Capua, *Life of Catherine* 366, p. 339.

Dying into the Mercy of the Trinity

In a very special way, our Blessed Mother will be with us and our loved ones as we face death, just as she has been with us so lovingly throughout our lives: "Holy Mary, Mother of God, pray for us now, and at the hour of our death." St. John Damascene tells us that our Blessed Mother's own death was a tender "falling asleep, a homecoming."[215] We see in her peaceful death the pledge of our fulfillment. This is *our* destiny: "How has death come to be regarded simply as an everyday sleep? Fear is gone, no longer haunting the little ones in Christ."[216] Through the grace of her Son, our Blessed Mother's death was sweet, and so it is meant to be for all of us, her children, "whose death is now called blessed."[217]

In the tenderness of her death, the Mother of the Lord has shown us how to die in the arms of her beloved Son. In our Blessed Mother, death was stripped of its horror, and was "shown to be a joy." St. John Damascene pictures the apostles gathered around her holy bedside, singing tenderly to her the sweetest of hymns, accompanied by "the harp of the Spirit."[218] Hosts of angels were present, filling the room with heavenly melodies that "only angels can sing," as they bore her precious soul to heaven.[219] In our funeral liturgies, we sing with deep emotion, "May the angels lead you into paradise." In union with our Blessed Mother, we,

---

[215] St. John Damascene, "On the Dormition," Homily 1, in *On the Dormition of Mary*, p. 195.

[216] St. Andrew of Crete, "On the Dormition of the Mother of God," Homily 3, in *On the Dormition of Mary*, p. 140.

[217] St. John Damascene, "On the Dormition," Homily 1, in *On the Dormition of Mary*, p. 197.

[218] Ibid., pp. 196, 197.

[219] St. John Damascene, "On the Dormition of the Mother of God," Homily 2, in *On the Dormition of Mary*, pp. 211, 214, 215.

too, can trust that that the angels will be present with us, and with our loved ones, surrounding us with their heavenly singing as they bear our souls gently home to heaven.

At the bedside of our dying loved ones, we are on holy ground (Exod. 3:5; Acts 7:33). Regardless of the circumstances, no one dies alone. Most intimately, the Father, the Lord Jesus, and the Holy Spirit are there, enfolding our loved ones in Their sacred embrace, bidding them to say yes to Their love with all the power of their souls. Our Blessed Mother is also there, as well as countless saints, angels, and unseen loved ones, invisibly helping and preparing the ones we love to give themselves to the Trinity and to be welcomed home. Let us do all that we can to help our loved ones entrust their souls to the gentle arms of the Father, in union with the Lord Jesus: "Father, into Your hands I commend my spirit" (Luke 23:46). If it is the Trinity's plan of love for us to be present at a loved one's death, the sacred intimacy of that moment is beyond the power of words to describe. This is the moment for which our loved one has been created, the moment to which everything in his or her life has been leading: "It is finished" (John 19:30). What awaits our loved one is the ecstasy of heaven.

The death of loved ones, and our sacred time with them, changes us. In our grief, there begins to be also a paradoxical joy, as we are drawn to pray not only for but also to them. We start to experience intimately their closeness, their love and gratitude, their tender care for us. As St. Ambrose beautifully notes, a place within us begins to live in heaven, where our loved ones dwell, and death no longer seems like a stranger to us.[220]

---

[220] St. Ambrose, *On the Death of Satyrus* I.6.

Dying into the Mercy of the Trinity

More than ever, we realize that, soon enough, we, too, will come to the moment of our death, and we will do so in complete helplessness. As St. Thérèse was dying, she confessed her own struggles: "I never stop moaning and groaning; I'm crying all the time.... My God, I can't stand it anymore! Have pity on me."[221] And yet, Thérèse assures us, our very weakness will be our joy: "How happy I am to see myself imperfect."[222] "What pleases Him is that He sees me loving my littleness and my poverty, the blind hope I have in His mercy."[223]

Our loved ones who have gone before us surely are now praying for us, that we may live each day with trust in the Trinity's mercy and in self-giving love for the Trinity and for one another. We believe and trust that our deceased loved ones will be tenderly with us at our death, and that, in their loving presence, the prayer of St. John of the Cross will be fulfilled one day in us: "May the vision of Your beauty be my death." Living for the Trinity's glory now, may we hear at our death the Lord's tender invitation to us: "Arise, my beautiful one, and come" (Song of Sol. 2:10).[224]

---

[221] St. Thérèse of Lisieux, *Her Last Conversations*, p. 193.

[222] Ibid., p. 116.

[223] St. Thérèse of Lisieux, Letter 197, in *Letters*, vol. 2, p. 999.

[224] St. John of the Cross, *The Spiritual Canticle* 11.10; 39.8, pp. 452, 560.

5

Living in Heaven on Earth

In this final chapter, we reflect on the magnificent truth that we do not have to wait for death in order to savor the joys of heaven. The Trinity's love has provided us with the means to begin living in heaven here on earth. Heaven is the Blessed Trinity, and wherever the Divine Persons are, there is heaven. Scripture proclaims to us the profound truth that the Trinity dwell within *us*: "Those who love me will keep my word, and my Father will love them, and we will come to them and make our home with them" (John 14:23). "Your body is a temple of the Holy Spirit within you" (1 Cor. 6:19). "God's temple is holy, and you are that temple" (1 Cor. 3:17). These and other Scriptural passages have drawn the saints to savor heaven here on earth by living deeply in the presence of the Trinity within them.

This tremendous blessing is meant for every one of us. Meditating on Luke 17:21, "The Kingdom of God is within you," St. John of the Cross cries out, "O soul ... so anxious to know the dwelling place of your Beloved ... you yourself are His dwelling.... This is something of immense gladness for you, to see that all your good is so close to you as to be within you."[225]

---

[225] St. John of the Cross, *The Spiritual Canticle* I.7, p. 418.

St. Thomas Aquinas assures us that the heart of heaven is enjoying the Blessed Trinity,[226] and this immeasurable blessing is already ours through three precious gifts: sanctifying grace, the Eucharist, and the virtue of charity. Sanctifying grace, poured into our souls at our Baptisms, is "the beginning of everlasting glory in us."[227] The Eucharist, which inebriates us with "sweetness of divine goodness," is the cause and foretaste of eternal life in us: "Those who eat my flesh and drink my blood have eternal life" (John 6:54).[228] And the virtue of charity, enkindled in us by the Eucharist, is the very heart of the everlasting life of heaven.[229]

The Divine Persons Dwell in Us through Grace

We consider first the precious gift of sanctifying grace, bestowed on us through Baptism. How blessed we would be if we truly appreciated the treasures the Divine Persons pour into our souls when we are baptized! "From His fullness we have all received, grace upon grace" (John 1:16). Through Baptism we become members of the Lord's Mystical Body, with the Trinity infusing into our souls the magnificent gifts of sanctifying grace, the supernatural virtues, and the seven gifts of the Holy Spirit, all flowing from the Lord, our Head, to us.[230] When St. Cyril of Jerusalem explained to the newly initiated Christians the miracles they had experienced through Baptism, he assured them that through this wondrous sacrament, paradise itself had been opened to them.[231]

---

[226] St. Thomas Aquinas, *Summa Theologiae* II-II.18.2, ad. 2.
[227] Ibid., II–II.24.3, ad. 2.
[228] Ibid., III.79.1, ad. 2; III.79.2.
[229] Ibid., II-II.23.3; III.73.3, ad. 3.
[230] Ibid., III.69.4; I-II.68.5.
[231] St. Cyril of Jerusalem, *Catechetical Lectures* 19.9.

Living in Heaven on Earth

Indeed, through sanctifying grace bestowed on us in this sacrament, we now dwell in a profound way in paradise, for at Baptism the Divine Persons come to dwell intimately in our souls.[232] St. Thomas Aquinas tells us that sanctifying grace is a supernatural quality, a wondrous habit that elevates our souls, giving them a created participation in the very life of the Trinity.[233] Through sanctifying grace we are intimately united to the Divine Persons, who *are* Heaven. It is Their sweet presence within us that enables us to taste the joys of heaven here on earth.[234]

The Lord Himself tells us that He and His Father, and therefore the Holy Spirit as well, will come to us and make Their home within us (John 14:23). Through the precious gift of sanctifying grace, the Father, the Son, and the Holy Spirit give Themselves completely to us, to dwell intimately within us, not as our Creator, but in an entirely new way, as intimately *beloved* to us.[235] What joy and peace would be ours if we truly realized the priceless treasure we bear within us! The God of heaven and earth, the Divine Persons of the Trinity, who are beauty, goodness, tenderness, mercy, and love, dwell within us and make us Their sweet and intimate home through the gift of sanctifying grace.

Furthermore, every time there is an increase of sanctifying grace or infused virtue in our souls, all Three Divine Persons deepen their presence in us.[236] In a special way, when charity, which is a created participation in the Holy Spirit, is increased in our wills, the intimate presence of the Holy Spirit is deepened

---

[232] St. Thomas Aquinas, *Summa Theologiae* I.43.5; I.43.4, ad. 2.
[233] Ibid., I-II.110.2, 4; 112.1.
[234] Ibid., I.43.5.
[235] Ibid.
[236] Ibid., I.43.6, ad. 2

in our souls.[237] Inseparably, when a "sweet" knowledge of the Trinity—a knowing that breaks forth into love—is increased in our minds, the presence of God the Son, the Word who eternally breathes forth the Spirit of love, is deepened within us.[238] We experience this "sweet knowledge," for example, when we read or hear a Scripture passage, or understand more profoundly a truth of our Faith, in such a way that our heart is inflamed with deeper love of the Trinity.

Since the Divine Persons of the Trinity are one God, when the presence of one Person is deepened in us, so, also, is the intimate presence of the other two Persons. Even more, when Their presence is bestowed or deepened in us through sanctifying grace, They give Themselves to us without reserve.[239] They do this for an astounding reason: so that they may dwell within us and make our souls Their home and heaven, enabling us to "possess" and "enjoy" Them as our very own.[240]

We learn by experience that the Persons of the Trinity live within us to fill us with Their "sweetness, refreshment, and consolation." The Father tenderly told St. Catherine of Siena, "I call the soul 'heaven' because I make heaven wherever I dwell by grace."[241] As Catherine herself grew to savor the Trinity's presence within her, she would cry out in worship and praise, "You, Eternal Trinity, are a deep sea. The more I enter You, the more I discover, and the more I discover, the more I seek You."[242] Catherine's example

----

[237] Ibid., I.43.5, ad. 2.

[238] Ibid.

[239] Ibid., I.43.4, ad. 1.

[240] Ibid., I.43.2; I.43.3.

[241] St. Catherine of Siena, Letter 73, in *Letters*, vol. 1, p. 227; *The Dialogue* 33, p. 75.

[242] St. Catherine of Siena, *The Dialogue* 167, p. 364.

encourages us to rest often in the Trinity's loving presence within us, and in this way to find heaven in our souls.

Perhaps no other saint so strongly urges us to live consciously in the presence of the Trinity dwelling within us than St. John of the Cross. He reminds us that when we truly love someone, there is nothing we desire as much as our loved one's intimate presence and companionship.[243] St. Augustine's words to the Lord, "I sought You outside of myself, but all the while You were within me,"[244] so deeply touched St. John that he begs us to dwell "within" our souls, where the Divine Persons intimately live. May our souls be ever more deeply the Trinity's sweet heaven! Throughout the day, in our work and our rest, in our successes and failures, in our sufferings and joys, may we adore the Trinity, who make Their home within us.[245] May we savor the Trinity's presence especially through contemplative prayer, taking time daily to repose in the Divine Persons' presence. By practices such as gently repeating a phrase that the Holy Spirit may place in our hearts, we can grow in the habit of prayer that draws us to rest more deeply in the Trinity dwelling in our souls, and thus to taste the joys of heaven even now.

The Eucharist: Foretaste of Heaven

Our loving reception of the Lord in the Eucharist is the most intimate way in which the Trinity allow us to taste heaven on earth. This precious sacrament truly is the "pledge of future glory."[246]

---

[243] St. John of the Cross, *The Spiritual Canticle* 36.1, p. 545.

[244] St. Augustine, *Confessions* 10.27.

[245] St. John of the Cross, *The Spiritual Canticle* I.10, p. 419.

[246] Feast of Corpus Christi, Magnificat antiphon for Second Vespers, The Liturgy Archive, http://www.liturgies.net/Liturgies/Catholic/loh/corpuschristiep2.htm.

St. John Paul II describes with heartfelt emotion how we are raised to heaven when we are present at Mass, as we "become part of that great multitude which cries out: 'Salvation belongs to our God who is seated on the throne, and to the Lamb!' (Rev. 7:10)." As we are raised to heaven, heaven itself comes down to us. Indeed, the sacrament of the Eucharist, the most wondrous fruit of the Mass, is the sweetest taste and "glimpse of heaven on earth."[247]

In writing about her first Holy Communion, St. Thérèse tells us that "all the joy of Heaven" entered her heart when she received the Lord. Unable to hold back her tears, she realized that when she received the Lord in the Eucharist, "heaven itself" was in her soul.[248] St. Thomas Aquinas, too, tenderly contemplates the power of the Eucharist to raise us to heaven and to enable us to live in heaven here on earth. The Eucharist is the greatest of all the sacraments, the culmination and purpose of every other sacrament, precisely because in it we receive the precious Body and Blood of God the Son.[249] Because Jesus is "the Resurrection and the Life" (John 11:25), the Eucharist is the very cause of our eternal life in heaven: "Whoever eats of this Bread will live forever" (John 6:51).[250]

Since the Lord is the font of all grace (John 1:16), devoutly receiving the Eucharist also deepens sanctifying grace and charity within us, "inebriating" us with heavenly delight.[251] Meditating on the Scriptural words that "blood and water came out" of

---

[247] St. John Paul II, Encyclical Letter *Ecclesia de Eucharistia* (April 17, 2003), no. 19.
[248] St. Thérèse of Lisieux, *Story of a Soul*, pp. 77, 78.
[249] St. Thomas Aquinas, *Summa Theologiae* III.65.3; III.63.6; III.73.3.
[250] Ibid., III.79.2.
[251] Ibid., III.79.1, ad. 2.

the pierced side of the crucified Lord (John 19:34), St. Thomas Aquinas reiterates the sentiments of St. John Chrysostom: "When you draw near to the awe-inspiring chalice, approach as if you were going to drink from Christ's own side."[252]

St. Thomas Aquinas loved the Lord's beautiful words at the Last Supper, at which He instituted the sacrament of the Eucharist: "I do not call you servants any longer ... but I have called you friends" (John 15:15). We naturally want to spend time with a beloved friend, and only our friend's physical presence is enough to content our heart. In a special way, we treasure deeply the presence and final words of a beloved friend. It is at this precious time, when a loved one is about to die, that his or her words are seared into our memory, and our most profound affection is enkindled deep in our soul. This is why the Lord chose to give us the sacrament of His most sacred Body and Blood at the Last Supper, before He was about to suffer His Passion and death for us.[253]

Having become man for our sake, the Lord has given us the exquisite gift of His physical presence in the Eucharist as a source of strength and comfort now, until we can enjoy His physical presence in an unhindered way in heaven. He imparts to us this sacred gift here on earth, uniting us to Himself most intimately in the Eucharist: "Those who eat my flesh, and drink my blood, abide in me, and I in them." (John 6:56). This most wondrous of all the sacraments gives us the intimate and "familiar" physical presence of the Lord, as the sign of the Lord's supreme charity for us.[254] The Lord surrenders Himself to us in this precious sacrament of the Eucharist ultimately so that, through it, He may

[252] Ibid., III.79.1.
[253] Ibid., III.73.5.
[254] Ibid., III.75.1.

bring us to heaven, where we will enjoy Him as the angels do, by the unhindered vision of His beauty.[255]

St. John Paul II concludes his encyclical letter on the Eucharist by quoting St. Thomas Aquinas, whom he calls the "impassioned poet of Christ in the Eucharist."[256] In his Corpus Christi hymn for Lauds, with its concluding verses used for Benediction, "O Salutaris," St. Thomas glorifies the Lord for giving Himself to us as our intimate companion, our daily food, and our heavenly reward. In his poetic sequence for the Mass of Corpus Christi, Thomas cries out, "O Jesus, Bread of Angels, make us see Your Good in the land of the living. You who feed us here, make us *there* the intimate companions of the saints." Becoming "companions of the saints" is a grace the Lord bestows on us even now through the Eucharist. In this most precious sacrament, the Lord gives us Himself as a "foretaste" of the eternal joys of heaven.[257] Moreover, in a profound way, He also gives us communion with those in heaven. St. John Damascene writes that the Eucharist is called "Holy Communion" because in receiving the Lord's precious Body and Blood, we communicate with and are intimately united to the Lord Jesus. Since those of us on earth and the blessed in heaven are members of His Mystical Body, in the Eucharist, therefore, we also "communicate with and are united to one another."[258]

This truth deeply touched St. Thérèse. She was convinced that, because those in heaven are one Mystical Body with the Lord, when we receive the Lord in the Eucharist, our loved ones

---

[255] Ibid., III.80.2, ad. 1 and 3.

[256] St. John Paul II, *Ecclesia de Eucharistia* 62.

[257] Pope Benedict XVI, Post-Synodal Exhortation *Sacramentum Caritatis* (March 13, 2007), no. 31.

[258] St. John Damascene, *On the Orthodox Faith* 4.3.

in heaven also are present to us in a very profound way. Thérèse writes of her own beautiful experience at her first Holy Communion: "Wasn't Heaven itself in my soul?" Yes. And because her saintly mother surely was in heaven, Thérèse tells us, "In receiving Jesus' visit, I received also Mamma's. She blessed me and rejoiced at my happiness."[259] What profound consolation for us! When we receive the Lord in the Eucharist, we can also commune with our loved ones who have died and who surely come to us united to their beloved Lord.

In the Eucharist, the Lord unites us to the faithful here on earth as well as to those in heaven. St. John Chrysostom urges us to come with profound faith and love to the Table of the Eucharist, where the gifts are not only joy but also "harmony, peace, and union of soul."[260] When we devoutly receive the Lord in the Eucharist, we receive also the grace to be more closely united to those we love here on earth, in a love that is itself a foretaste of heaven. This precious sacrament is thus the sacrament of the Church's unity,[261] for "the common spiritual good" of the entire Church is contained in the Lord given to us in the Eucharist.[262] The more lovingly we receive the Lord Jesus, the more united we become to those dear to us here on earth, especially to those with whom we are blessed to share the Eucharist. Our receiving of the Lord in this sacrament also unites us more deeply with all the members of the one Mystical Body of the Lord, in a foreshadowing of the loving union that will be ours in heaven.[263]

---

[259] St. Thérèse, *Story of a Soul*, p. 78.

[260] St. John Chrysostom, "On the Sacred Night of the Pasch, the Easter Vigil," in Toal, *Sunday Sermons*, vol. 2, p. 201.

[261] St. Thomas Aquinas, *Summa Theologiae* III.83.4, ad. 3.

[262] Ibid., III.65.3, ad. 1.

[263] Ibid., III.73.4.

Another wonderful effect of the Eucharist is a deepening in our souls of a profound spiritual delight and "sweetness" that allow us to taste heavenly joy even now: "Taste and see that the LORD is good" (Ps. 34:8).[264] This deep contentment, even in the midst of trials, continues after we receive the Eucharist and especially can be savored when we spend time in adoration of the Lord in the Blessed Sacrament. St. John Paul II tells us of his own intimate experience: "It is pleasant to spend time with him, to lie close to his breast like the beloved disciple (John 13:25) and to feel the infinite love present in his heart." The pope reminds us of how much every one of us truly needs this time in adoration and love before the Lord in the Blessed Sacrament. "How often, dear brothers and sisters, have I experienced this, and drawn from it strength, consolation and support!"[265]

Still another wondrous fruit of devoutly receiving the Lord in the Eucharist is a deepening of the presence of the entire Trinity within us. "I am in the Father and the Father is in me" (John 14:10). And where the Father and the Son are, there also is the Holy Spirit. Although it is the Lord Jesus who comes to us sacramentally, the presence of the entire Trinity thus deepens in our souls when we receive the Eucharist. The power of this sacrament is so great that even when we are unable to receive it but long to do so, grace is increased in our souls, and we become even more dearly the home and heaven of the Trinity.[266]

St. Catherine of Siena recounts how, during the Consecration at Mass, she "tasted the depths of the Trinity."[267] Surely

---

[264] Ibid., III.79.8, ad 2; 79.1.
[265] St. John Paul II, *Ecclesia de Eucharistia* 25.
[266] St. Thomas Aquinas, *Summa Theologiae* III.79.1, ad. 1; III.80.11.
[267] St. Catherine of Siena, *The Dialogue* 111, p. 210.

this was the grace given to her every time she desired to receive the Lord, which was daily. She assures us that this blessing can be ours. So, too, when we receive the Eucharist, the "power" of this sacrament, which is the "warmth of divine charity," remains deep within our souls.[268]

The Heavenly Virtue of Charity

The kindling of charity within us: this is an abiding effect of devoutly receiving the Lord in the Eucharist.[269] St. Thomas Aquinas calls the Eucharist "the sacrament of Charity," for in it we receive God the Son, whose very nature is love and whose presence within us inflames us with love.[270] We were created to enjoy the Trinity; charity not only leads us to this heavenly goal but also allows us to attain this goal even now. The greatest of all the virtues (1 Cor. 13:13), charity unites us intimately to the Trinity, giving us the power to love and enjoy the Divine Persons for Their own sake, and enabling us with great contentment to "rest" in Them.[271]

Disposing "all things well" (Wisd. 8:1), the Trinity flood our souls at Baptism with grace and the supernatural virtues, and especially with charity, which is a created participation in the Holy Spirit, whose very name is Love.[272] This precious virtue inclines our wills strongly, easily, and sweetly to love the Trinity above all else, and everyone else for the sake of the Trinity.[273] Because charity enables us to act with the Trinity's unselfish

---

[268] Ibid., 112, p. 211.
[269] St. Thomas Aquinas, *Summa Theologiae*, III.79.4.
[270] Ibid., III.73.3, ad. 3.
[271] Ibid., II-II.23.5, ad. 2; II-II.23.6.
[272] Ibid., II-II.24.7.
[273] Ibid., II-II.23.2; II-II.23.1, ad. 2.

love, no other virtue fills us with such exquisite delight or gives us such a sweet taste of heaven.[274] How many times we have experienced this truth when we have spent time with the Lord in adoration or drawn from the Trinity the grace to forgive, or to act with unselfish love!

To illumine further the heavenly beauty of the virtue of charity, St. Thomas Aquinas turns to the profound words of the Lord at the Last Supper: "I do not call you servants any longer ...; I have called you friends" (John 15:15). A true friendship, Thomas tells us, requires mutual, self-giving love that desires and works for the true good of our beloved friend. Furthermore, it entails a closeness based on a deep sharing and communication between us. This is the friendship-love that the Blessed Trinity have for us, since the Divine Persons communicate to us the best of all possible goods: Their very own intimate happiness.[275]

The virtue of charity shares in this friendship-love of the Trinity for us, enabling us to love the Trinity, and inseparably, one another, with the very same charity.[276] Before developing this profound insight, St. Thomas contemplates first how loving ourselves with the virtue of charity is the foundation of our being able to love others with the same heavenly charity. When we truly love ourselves, we desire and labor to attain for ourselves the very best good: intimate union with the Trinity. Because we know that the Divine Persons make Their home in our souls, we are peaceful and happy in our own company. Free of worry about our past, we are content with our present and have no fear of the future.[277]

---

[274] Ibid., II-II.23.2.
[275] Ibid., II-II.23.1.
[276] Ibid., II-II.25.1.
[277] Ibid., II-II.25.7.

Living in Heaven on Earth

Loving ourselves with the contentment of this true charity, we cannot help loving others in the same way and for the same reason. Through charity, we pray and labor by our self-giving love and service for the ultimate purpose that others, too, may attain the same "fellowship" (1 Cor. 1:9) of everlasting happiness that we desire for ourselves. This sharing in the Trinity's heavenly bliss is the deepest good that we want for all those we love with the virtue of charity.[278]

"You are the body of Christ and individually members of it" (1 Cor. 12:27). "God has so arranged the body … that the members may have the same care for one another" (1 Cor. 12:24–25). St. Paul gives us a profound description of the charity with which we are obliged to love one another as members of this one Body of Christ. Charity's love is "patient and kind, not jealous, arrogant, or rude." It does not seek its own interests, nor does it hold grudges or brood over injuries. Charity "bears all things, believes all things, endures all things." This greatest of all the virtues "never ends" (see 1 Cor. 13:4–8).

As she meditated on Paul's beautiful words, St. Catherine of Siena was inspired to picture all of us as bound together by the Trinity with the wondrous "chain of charity." Catherine recalls a fundamental truth of our existence: each of us individually is a part of the Body, not the whole of it. We have been created by the Trinity to *need* one another, just as our feet need our legs, and our hands need our arms. Catherine was convinced that the Trinity have irrevocably bound us to one another in this way precisely so that we will be "forced" to practice here on earth the beautiful virtue of charity, which is the very life of heaven.[279]

---

[278] Ibid., II-II.25.2, ad. 2.
[279] St. Catherine of Siena, *The Dialogue* 148, p. 311.

Sacred Scripture assures us that we cannot love God, whom we do not see, if we do not love our brothers and sisters, whom we do see (1 John 4:20). Church Fathers contemplated the profound implications of this truth in light of our being the one Body of the Lord, bound together by charity and receiving together the Lord's precious Body and Blood in the Eucharist. Countless saints have labored on behalf of the poor and have preached with great power on the sacred obligation we have to care for one another as members of the Lord's Mystical Body. St. John Chrysostom, for example, admonished those who made a display of honoring the precious Body and Blood of the Lord in church, but then despised His Body, their brothers and sisters in need, as they begged for food in the streets.[280] He praised the generosity of those who adorned the altar that holds the Lord's sacred Body and Blood but urged them to show the same generosity in caring for the poor. The altar, made of stone, is rightfully reverenced as holy. The poor, however, are worthy of even deeper reverence, for they do not simply hold the Lord's Body: they *are* the Lord's Body.[281]

Other Church Fathers, such as St. Gregory of Nazianzus, stress that the love and care that we give to one another, especially the most weak and vulnerable among us, will be the real treasures that we take with us into heaven. The Lord Himself assures us that whatever we do for the least of His brothers and sisters, we do for Him (Matt. 25:40). St. Gregory of Nazianzus reminds us that the very persons to whom we reach out to help in any way here on earth will be the very ones who welcome us into heaven's joy: "Let us show *Him* mercy in the persons of the

---

[280] St. John Chrysostom, *Commentary on First Corinthians* 27.6, 7.
[281] St. John Chrysostom, *Commentary on Second Corinthians* 20.3.

poor, so that when we come to leave this world *they* may receive us into eternal dwelling places."[282]

St. Catherine of Siena places before the eyes of our hearts an exquisite vision of heaven, whose very life is "joyous charity," and whose bliss we enter only through self-giving love.[283] There, in heaven, no selfish love exists, only the Trinitarian "familial charity in which each one shares in the good of the other."[284] Because charity's love "lasts eternally,"[285] Catherine urges us to live in heaven now by experiencing "through charity in this life what we shall see face to face in the next."[286] This is the charity that overflows from our Blessed Mother and shines in the angels and the saints, inspiring them to pray for us and to help us in our every need. Clothed in this same heavenly virtue, may we, too, be welcomed one day into the tender embrace of the Divine Persons, who are the heaven of self-giving love for which we have been made.

---

[282] St. Gregory of Nazianzus, *Oration 14: On the Love of the Poor* 40, in *Liturgy of the Hours*, vol. 2 (New York: Catholic Book Publishing, 1976), p. 267, emphasis added.

[283] St. Catherine of Siena, *The Dialogue* 148, p. 315.

[284] St. Catherine of Siena, Letter DT I, in *Letters*, vol. 2, p. 53.

[285] St. Catherine of Siena, *The Dialogue* 41, p. 84.

[286] St. Catherine of Siena, Letter DT I, in *Letters*, vol. 2, p. 53.

Select Bibliography

Ambrose of Milan, St. *On the Death of Satyrus*. Books 1 and 2. Translated by H. de Romestin, E. de Romestin, and H. T. F. Duckworth. In vol. 10 of *Nicene and Post-Nicene Fathers*. Second series. Edited by Philip Schaff and Henry Wace. Buffalo, NY: Christian Literature Publishing, 1896. Revised and edited for New Advent by Kevin Knight. http://www. newadvent.org/fathers/34031.htm.

———. *On the Death of Emperor Theodosius*. Translated by Roy J. Deferrari. In *Funeral Orations by Saint Gregory Nazianzen and Saint Ambrose*. Vol. 2 of *The Fathers of the Church*. Translated by Leo P. McCauley, S.J.; John J. Sullivan, C.S.Sp.; Martin R. P. McGuire; and Roy J. Deferrari. New York: Fathers of the Church, 1953.

Amphilochius of Iconium, St. "On the Holy Night of the Pasch, the Easter Vigil." In vol. 2 of *The Sunday Sermons of the Great Fathers*. Translated and edited by M. F. Toal, D.D. San Francisco: Ignatius Press, 1996.

"An Ancient Homily on Holy Saturday." The Liturgy Archive. http://www.liturgies.net/Liturgies/Catholic/loh/lent/holy saturdayor.htm

Andrew of Crete, St. "On the Dormition of the Mother of God," Homilies 1–3. In *On the Dormition of Mary: Early Patristic Homilies.* Translated by Brian E. Daley, S.J. Crestwood, NY: St. Vladimir's Seminary Press, 1998.

Augustine of Hippo, St. *City of God.* Translated by Marcus Dods. In vol. 2 of *Nicene and Post-Nicene Fathers*, First Series. Edited by Philip Schaff. Buffalo, New York: Christian Literature Publishing, 1887. Revised and edited for New Advent by Kevin Knight. http://www.newadvent.org/fathers/1201.htm.

—. *Confessions.* Translated by J.G. Pilkington. In vol. 1 of *Nicene and Post-Nicene Fathers*, First Series. Edited by Philip Schaff. Buffalo, NY: Christian Literature Publishing, 1887. Revised and edited for New Advent by Kevin Knight. http://www.newadvent.org/fathers/1101.htm.

—. *On the Trinity.* Translated by Arthur West Haddan. In vol. 3 of *Nicene and Post-Nicene Fathers*, First Series. Edited by Philip Schaff. Buffalo, New York: Christian Literature Publishing, 1887. Revised and edited for New Advent by Kevin Knight. http://www.newadvent.org/fathers/1301.htm.

—. *Tractates on the Gospel of John: 11–27.* Translated by John W. Rettig. In vol. 79 of *The Fathers of the Church.* Washington, D.C.: Catholic University of America Press, 1988.

—. *Tractates on the Gospel of John: 28–54.* Translated by John W. Rettig. In vol. 88 of *The Fathers of the Church.* Washington, D.C.: Catholic University of America Press, 1993.

—. *Tractates on the Gospel of John: 55–111.* Translated by John W. Rettig. In vol. 90 of *The Fathers of the Church.* Washington, D.C.: Catholic University of America Press, 1994.

Select Bibliography

Benedict XVI, Pope. Post-Synodal Exhortation *Sacramentum Caritatis* (March 13, 2007). Catholic Liturgical Library. http://www.catholicliturgy.com/index.cfm/FuseAction/Document.Contents/Index/2/SubIndex/0/DocumentIndex/557.

Bernard of Clairvaux, St. "Sermon 61 on the Song of Songs." Hymns and Chants. hymnsandchants.com/Texts/Sermons/SongOfSongs/SongsSermon61.htm.

———. Sermon 2. Office of Readings for the solemnity of All Saints. Liturgy Archive. The Liturgy Archive. http://www.liturgies.net/saints/allsaints/officeofreadings.htm.

———. Sermon 12 on Psalm 91. Office of Readings for the feast of the Guardian Angels. The Liturgy Archive. http://www.liturgies.net/saints/guardianangels/officeofreadings.htm.

———. *Sermons on the Song of Songs.* In *Bernard of Clairvaux: Selected Works.* Translated by G. E. Evans. New York: Paulist Press, 1987.

Catherine of Siena, St. *The Dialogue.* Translated by Suzanne Noffke, O.P. New York: Paulist Press, 1980.

———. *The Letters of St. Catherine of Siena.* Vol. 1. Translated by Suzanne Noffke, O.P. Binghamton, New York: Medieval and Renaissance Texts and Studies, 1988.

———. *The Letters of St. Catherine of Siena.* Vol. 2. Translated by Suzanne Noffke, O.P. Tempe, Arizona: Center for Medieval and Renaissance Texts and Studies, 2001.

———. *The Letters of St. Catherine of Siena.* Vol. 4. Translated by Suzanne Noffke, O.P. Tempe, AZ: Arizona Center for Medieval and Renaissance Texts and Studies, 2008.

"Cherubic Hymn." "The Divine Liturgy: The Great Entrance." Byzantine Catholic Archeparchy of Pittsburgh. https://mci. archpitt.org/liturgy/Divine_Liturgy_Great_Entrance.html.

Cyprian, St. *On Mortality*. EWTN. https://www.ewtn.com/library/SOURCES/MORTAL.TXT.

Cyril of Jerusalem, St. Catechetical Lecture 19. Translated by Edwin Hamilton Gifford. In vol. 7 of *Nicene and Post-Nicene Fathers*, Second Series. Edited by Philip Schaff and Henry Wace. Buffalo, NY: Christian Literature Publishing, 1894. Revised and edited for New Advent by Kevin Knight. http://www.newadvent.org/fathers/310119.htm.

Fulgentius of Ruspe, St. Sermon 3. Office of Readings for the feast of St. Stephen. http://www.liturgies.net/saints/stephen/officeofreadings.htm.

Gregory of Nazianzus, St. "On the Holy Pasch: Second Sermon." In vol. 2 of *The Sunday Sermons of the Great Fathers*. Translated and edited by M. F. Toal, D.D. San Francisco: Ignatius Press, 1996.

———. *Oration 8: On His Sister, St. Gorgonia*. Translated by Charles Gordon Browne and James Edward Swallow. In vol. 7 of *Nicene and Post-Nicene Fathers*, Second Series. Edited by Philip Schaff and Henry Wace. Buffalo, New York: Christian Literature Publishing, 1894. Revised and edited for New Advent by Kevin Knight. http://www.newadvent.org/fathers/310208.htm.

———. *Oration 14: On the Love of the Poor*. In vol. 2 of *The Liturgy of the Hours*. New York: Catholic Book Publishing, 1976.

———. *Oration 18: On His Father*. Translated by Charles Gordon Browne and James Edward Swallow. In vol. 7 of *Nicene and*

Post-Nicene Fathers, Second Series. Edited by Philip Schaff and Henry Wace. Buffalo, New York: Christian Literature Publishing, 1894. Revised and edited for New Advent by Kevin Knight. http://www.newadvent.org/fathers/310218.htm.

———. *Oration 43: On St. Basil.* Translated by Charles Gordon Browne and James Edward Swallow. In vol. 7 of *Nicene and Post-Nicene Fathers*, Second Series. Edited by Philip Schaff and Henry Wace. Buffalo, New York: Christian Literature Publishing, 1894. Revised and edited for New Advent by Kevin Knight. http://www.newadvent.org/fathers/310243.htm.

Gregory of Nyssa, St. *On the Soul and the Resurrection.* Translated by Catharine Roth. Crestwood, NY: St. Vladimir's Seminary Press, 1993.

"Hymn to the Mother of God." In "Prayers to the Blessed Mother of God according to the Byzantine Rite Tradition." Byzantine Catholic Archeparchy of Pittsburgh. http://www.archpitt. org/prayers-to-the-blessed-mother-of-god-according-to-the-byzantine-rite-tradition/

John Chrysostom. St. "Homily 20 on Second Corinthians." Translated by Talbot W. Chambers. In vol. 12 of *Nicene and Post-Nicene Fathers*, First Series. Edited by Philip Schaff. Buffalo, New York: Christian Literature Publishing, 1889. Revised and edited for New Advent by Kevin Knight. http://www. newadvent.org/fathers/220220.htm.

———. "Homily 27 on First Corinthians." Translated by Talbot W. Chambers. In vol. 12 of *Nicene and Post-Nicene Fathers*, First Series. Edited by Philip Schaff. Buffalo, New York: Christian Literature Publishing, 1889. Revised and edited for New Advent by Kevin Knight. http:/www.newadvent. org/fathers/220127.htm.

———. *Commentary on Saint John the Apostle and Evangelist: Homilies 1–47*. Vol. 33 of *The Fathers of the Church*. Translated by Sister Thomas Aquinas Goggin, S.C.H. New York: Fathers of the Church, 1957.

———. "On the Sacred Night of the Pasch, the Easter Vigil." In vol. 2 of *The Sunday Sermons of the Great Fathers*. Translated and edited by M. F. Toal, D.D. San Francisco: Ignatius Press, 1996.

John Damascene, St. "On the Dormition of the Mother of God." Homily 1. In *On the Dormition of Mary: Early Patristic Homilies*. Translated by Brian E. Daley, S.J. Crestwood, NY: St. Vladimir's Seminary Press, 1998.

———. *An Exposition of the Orthodox Faith*. Translated by E. W. Watson and L. Pullan. In vol. 9 of *Nicene and Post-Nicene Fathers*, Second Series. Edited by Philip Schaff and Henry Wace. Buffalo, NY: Christian Literature Publishing, 1899. Revised and edited for New Advent by Kevin Knight. http:// www.newadvent.org/fathers/3304.htm.

John of the Cross, St. *The Collected Works of St. John of the Cross*. Translated by Kieran Kavanaugh, O.C.D., and Otilio Rodriguez, O.C.D. Washington, D.C.: Institute of Carmelite Studies, 1973.

John Paul II, St. Encyclical Letter *Ecclesia de Eucharistia* (April 17, 2003). Vatican website. http://www.vatican.va/ holy_father/special_features/encyclicals/documents/hf_jp-ii_ enc_20030417_ecclesia_eucharistia_en.html.

Select Bibliography

————. Apostolic Letter *Salvifici Dolores* (February 11, 1984). Vatican wesite. http://w2.vatican.va/content/john-paul-ii/en/apost_letters/1984/documents/hf_jp-ii_apl_11021984_salvifici-doloris.html.

————. "Christ's Words on the Resurrection Complete the Revelation of the Body." General Audience (December 16, 1981). EWTN website. http://www.ewtn.com/library/papaldoc/jp2tb67.htm.

Leo the Great, St. "On the Passion of Our Lord." In vol. 2 of *The Sunday Sermons of the Great Fathers*. Translated and edited by M. F. Toal, D.D. San Francisco: Ignatius Press, 1996.

Louis de Montfort, St. *True Devotion to Mary*. EWTN website. https://www.ewtn.com/library/Montfort/TRUEDEVO.HTM

Maximus, St. "On the Lord's Resurrection and the Prayer of the Good Thief." In vol. 2 of *The Sunday Sermons of the Great Fathers*. San Francisco: Ignatius Press, 1996.

Raymond of Capua, Bl. *The Life of Catherine of Siena*. Translated by Conleth Kearns, O.P. Wilmington, DE: Michael Glazier, 1980.

Thérèse of Lisieux. *Thérèse of Lisieux: Her Last Conversations*. Translated by John Clarke, O.C.D. Washington, D.C.: ICS Publications, 1977.

————. *Letters of St. Thérèse of Lisieux*. Vol. 1, *1877–1890*. Translated by John Clarke, O.C.D. Washington, D.C.: ICS Publications, 1982.

————. *Letters of St. Thérèse of Lisieux*. Vol. 2, *1890–1897*. Translated by John Clarke, O.C.D. Washington, D.C.: ICS Publications, 1988.

————. *Story of a Soul: The Autobiography of St. Thérèse of Lisieux*. Translated by John Clarke, O.C.D. Washington, D.C.: ICS Publications, 1972.

Thomas Aquinas, St. *Commentary on the Gospel of John*. Translated by Fabian Larcher, O.P., and James A. Weisheipl, O.P. Albany, NY: Magi Books, 1980. Priory of the Immaculate Conception at the Dominican House of Studies. https://dhspriory.org/thomas/SSJohn.htm.

————. "Life Everlasting." In *Commentary on the Apostles' Creed*. Translated by Joseph B. Collins. Edited by Joseph Kenny, O.P. New York, 1939. Priory of the Immaculate Conception at the Dominican House of Studies. https://dhspriory.org/thomas/Creed.htm#12.

————. *Summa Theologiae*. 2nd rev. ed. 1920. Translated by Fathers of the English Dominican Province. New Advent. http://home.newadvent.org/summa/.

"Troparion of Pascha." Byzantine Catholic Archeparchy of Pittsburgh. https://mci.archpitt.org/liturgy/Troparion of Pascha. html.

About the Author

Sr. Mary Ann Fatula, O.P., Ph.D., served as a professor of theology at Ohio Dominican University in Columbus, Ohio, and for more than thirty years taught theology there. Sr. Mary Ann is the author of *Catherine of Siena's Way*; *Holy Spirit, Unbounded Gift of Joy*; and *Thomas Aquinas, Preacher and Friend*.

Index of Scriptural Citations

Index of Scriptural Citations

Index of Names and Subjects

B

babies, 29, 36, 37, 38, 54, 78;
  risen bodies of babies who
  died, 53, 54; unbaptized
  babies, 37, 54n141; unborn
  babies, 29, 37, 53, 54, 57,
  78, 79
Baptism, 9, 16, 22, 36, 37, 79,
  86, 87, 95
Basil the Great, St., 24
Beatific Vision, 8, 59
beauty, of the created universe,
  59; of the Father, 10; of the
  Holy Spirit, 16; of the Lord,
  12, 92; of the risen body, 51,
  52, 57; of the Trinity, 3, 8,
  58, 59, 61, 83, 87
Bellière, Abbé Maurice, 32, 33,
  34, 35
Benediction, 92
Benedict XVI, Pope, 92n257
Bernard of Clairvaux, St., 6–7,
  13, 17, 42
Blessed Sacrament, 94
Blood of Jesus, x, 12, 65, 68, 69,
  71, 80, 90, 91, 92, 98
body, 15, 49, 50, 85; of our
  Blessed Mother, 51, 59; created to be a gift, 30; of the
  Lord, 47, 51; of the Lord in
  the Eucharist, x, 12, 80, 90,

91, 92, 98; risen body, 45, 46,
  50-57, 61; risen body of the
  Lord, 12, 46, 47, 52, 56, 57,
  59, 61; spousal meaning, 15;
  temple of the Holy Spirit, 85
burial, 23, 50

C

Cana, wedding feast of, 14
Catechism of the Catholic Church,
  22n53, 29n73, 36, 37, 46,
  51, 54n141, 63, 70, 76, 77,
  79, 80
Catherine of Siena, St., 7,
  12n25, 14n30, 21n50, 22n52,
  24n57, 25, 26, 27, 31, 32,
  37n97, 40, 42, 43n114,
  49n127, 52n135, 52n137, 67,
  68, 69, 70, 71, 72, 73n197,
  76, 77, 78, 79n212, 80, 88,
  94, 97, 99
Cecilia, St., 28
Céline Martin, sister of St.
  Thérèse, 38, 39
cemetery, consecrated, 23, 50
charity, virtue of, x, 21, 22,
  23, 31, 40, 42, 47, 86, 87,
  90, 91, 95–99; binding us
  together in heaven, 40, 99;
  enkindled by the Eucha-
  rist, 86, 90, 95; foretaste

Index of Names and Subjects

heaven, 3; closeness to the saints and angels in heaven, 21–43; closeness to the Trinity in heaven, 3–20; communicating with one another in heaven, 39–40; heaven is the Trinity, 3–20; heaven on earth, 85–99; living in heaven now through closeness to deceased loved ones, 24–25; as our wedding feast, 14; reunion with loved ones in heaven, 37–40, 42; sharing in the Father's and Son's breathing forth of the Holy Spirit, 18

hell, 70

help, for one another, 22, 78, 82, 98; from those in heaven, 31–35; medical, 79; psychological, 79; spiritual, 77, 79

helplessness, 83

Holy Communion, 92

Holy Innocents, 54

Holy Saturday, 13, 47n119

Holy Spirit, 3, 4, 6, 15–20, 22; breathed forth eternally by the Father and the Son, 18; Comforter, 18; delight of the Father and the Son, 6; Divine Person who is love, 6,

15–16; fountain of love, 16; gift given to be enjoyed and possessed, 16–17; intimacy with the Holy Spirit, 15–19; joy given by the Holy Spirit, 16, 18; kiss of the Father and the Son, 7, 17–18; love of the Father and the Son, 6–7, 15–16; receiving all that He is from the Father and the Son, 6; our closeness in heaven to the Holy Spirit, 15–19; permeating our risen bodies, 47, 52; Spirit of the Father, 6; Spirit of the Son, 6; sweetness of the Father and the Son, 6; tenderness of, 17, 18

hope, 64, 65, 69, 70, 71, 72

hospice, 80

human beings, meaning as gift, 15, 30; spousal meaning, 14

humility, 35, 42, 68

hurts, 79

hydration, to preserve life, 76

hymns, 60, 81

I

illness, 53

immortality, of human soul, 52 of risen body, 52, 53

Index of Names and Subjects

Father for us, 8–11; heroic,
74; in heaven, 37, 99; of the
Holy Spirit for us, 15–19; of
Jesus for us, 11–15, 91–92; the
Lord's redemptive love, 73;
Person of the Holy Spirit, 6,
15, 16; for one another, 21–24,
42, 43, 97–99; of the saints
for us, 31–32; for the Trinity,
19; the Trinity's love for us,
19–20, 78, 88
loveliness of the created world,
58–60
Luke the Evangelist, St., 15, 63,
64, 71

M

Macrina, St., 49, 50
married love, 14, 42
Martha, St., 65
Martin, Céline, sister of St.
Thérèse, 38, 39
Martin, Léonie, sister of St.
Thérèse, 39
Martin, Pauline, sister of St.
Thérèse, 34
Martin, St. Louis, father of St.
Thérèse, 26, 38
Martin, St. Zélie, mother of St.
Thérèse, 26, 38

Mary Magdalene, St., 11, 27, 36,
69
Mary, Mother of Jesus and
our Mother, 19, 31, 32, 33,
50–51, 57, 81; Assumption,
50, 51; death, 50–51, 81;
love, prayer, and care for us,
31–32, 81
Mary, St., sister of Lazarus, 65
Mass, 12, 22, 40, 41, 90, 94
Maximus, St., 48, 71n191,
71n193
medication, pain-relieving, 76
mercy, 71, 98; of Jesus, 34–35,
66, 67–68, 72, 83; of the
saints, 35–37; of the Trinity,
36, 67–72
Michael the Archangel, St., 41,
80
mind, 88
miracles, 16
Monica, St., 66
mother, 10
movement in heaven, 54–55
music, 60
Mystical Body of the Lord
Jesus, 9, 10, 48, 64, 86, 92,
93, 98
mystical marriage of the Lord
with us, 14

Index of Names and Subjects

Index of Names and Subjects

V
vigor, 53
virtues, 43, 86

W
weakness, 28, 35, 53, 54, 68, 83
will, 87, of the Trinity for us, 67
worry, 96

wounds, 13, 18, 29, 36, 37, 39,
43; of Jesus, 13
wrongs, 37

Y
youthfulness, 53, 54

Sophia Institute

Sophia Institute is a nonprofit institution that seeks to nurture the spiritual, moral, and cultural life of souls and to spread the Gospel of Christ in conformity with the authentic teachings of the Roman Catholic Church.

Sophia Institute Press fulfills this mission by offering translations, reprints, and new publications that afford readers a rich source of the enduring wisdom of mankind.

Sophia Institute also operates two popular online Catholic resources: CrisisMagazine.com and CatholicExchange.com.

Crisis Magazine provides insightful cultural analysis that arms readers with the arguments necessary for navigating the ideological and theological minefields of the day. *Catholic Exchange* provides world news from a Catholic perspective as well as daily devotionals and articles that will help you to grow in holiness and live a life consistent with the teachings of the Church.

In 2013, Sophia Institute launched Sophia Institute for Teachers to renew and rebuild Catholic culture through service to Catholic education. With the goal of nurturing the spiritual, moral, and cultural life of souls, and an abiding respect for the role and work of teachers, we strive to provide materials and programs that are at once enlightening to the mind and ennobling to the heart; faithful and complete, as well as useful and practical.

Sophia Institute gratefully recognizes the Solidarity Association for preserving and encouraging the growth of our apostolate over the course of many years. Without their generous and timely support, this book would not be in your hands.

www.SophiaInstitute.com
www.CatholicExchange.com
www.CrisisMagazine.com
www.SophiaInstituteforTeachers.org

Sophia Institute Press® is a registered trademark of Sophia Institute.
Sophia Institute is a tax-exempt institution as defined by the
Internal Revenue Code, Section 501(c)(3). Tax I.D. 22-2548708.